How Corporate America Amass Revenue & Growth

Dr. Ebenezer A. Robinson, Ph.D.

DEDICATION

This book is dedicated to the Lord Jesus Christ. The Lord Jesus Christ is my GOD and my SAVIOR. I worship, praise, and thank you Lord Jesus Christ for the gift of eternal life. Thank you for standing by me every step of the way. Glory be to GOD the Father.

CONTENTS

ACKNOWLEDGMENTS

I would like to take this opportunity to express my heartfelt gratitude to all who helped me complete this book. Their comments and suggestions were a large part of the success of this book. I am also extremely appreciative of my children and entire family. I would like to thank my late mom and dad, who always had faith in everything I did. I wish they were here to share in this achievement. Finally, I would like to thank all my friends, Facebook friends and family, and people at Church, work, coffee shops, stores, and the public at large, for their support, patience, and listening to my endless rapports about this book over a period of years, without wish I could never have completed this book. Thank you all for believing in me.

CHAPTER 1
Compendium of Corporate America Management Concepts

This book contain a compendium of fortune 500 industries to showcase. In Corporate America, several managers prefer to introduce new products in order to enhance the living standard of the society and then maximize revenue. In this book, you will peruse how excellent organizations are always changing and evolving to find the best competitive position. But this does not happen unless senior management is focused on innovation, allows time for changes to be implemented, financially supports change and finally is willing to take calculated risks. There are going to be times when changes and innovations are not going to be successful and senior management must be willing to accept the cost of these risks if unsuccessful. Secondly, the truly good leaders usually are those that can surround themselves with a strong executive team and share their management powers with this team. Unless a firm is in a turnaround situation participative management is normally the best style to use.

This book will discuss two different theories that both yield positive results and eventually intersect and enhance each other. This manuscript will logically cover the main issues, associated concerns, improvement areas and provide a detailed supposition on the contrasting styles and approaches of change. Obviously there is more than one way to accomplish success, move a company forward and/or revamp a business process. Two theories that have a track record of attainment are Theories E and O. These two theories focus on very different goals to achieve realization and use a different approach to get there. Theory E's main goal is to maximize shareholder value, thus putting the emphasis and objectives towards an external concentration. Leadership manages and implements policy, processes and procedure from top to bottom. The focus is on structure and systems, enhancement and refining to realize maximum efficiency. The main process is to plan and establish programs to manage daily operations. The rewards system's motivation is financial in nature and consultants analyze problems and sell solutions. Theory O's concentration is centered on organizational capability, relying on internal application. Management effectively leads and encourages participation bottom up by engaging employees and considering feedback. Specific importance is placed on building a culture of positive behaviors and attitudes that create esprit decor. The process significance is to experiment and evolve to locate the method, course and procedure that works. The reward system is a motivational concept intended to build commitment and make available an honest day's pay for an honest day's work. Consultants reinforce management's ideas and shapes solutions to problems, rather than forcing a particular determination. Combined, these theories embrace economic value and organizational capabilities, set direction from the top and encourage individuals below, utilize systems and organizational concepts to create a (people) culture, uses incentives and consultants.

To increase shareholders interest, the no nonsense approach is to perform a 'hostile takeover' of sorts. If the goals are that clearly defined and do not take into account the livelihood on individuals, the objectives are to create efficiencies by any means necessary. This may include major overhauls of people, equipment and dated practices. On the other hand, reformation of corporate structure can also be achieved by transforming behaviors, values, principles and competencies designed to improve organizational capabilities, thus enhancing economic value. Top down management has its place and requires minimum involvement and input from staff. Lead, follow or get out of the way is the philosophy used to levy this style of leadership. Opposite, when participation is solicited and employees are connected to improving performance; teams are encouraged to create ways to enhance the work experience. Structures and systems being the immediate focus is considered the hard approach in moving forward. Outsourcing and eliminating practices and positions considered wasteful are imminent targets of deletion; the bottom-line is to increase the bottom-line. In contrast, building up the culture, behavior and attitude of workers offers an alternative means of increasing profits.

A clear corporate focus that ensures internal coordination throughout the business cycle and relies on decisive action to motivate and mobilize change, or an ability to organically grow over a period of time are two distinct process delivery systems to implore effective change. Rewards are proven ways to motivate, inspire and cultivate loyal personnel that come to accomplish task to the highest level of detail are critical to retention and achievement. Money is a great motivator, but will not sustain the appropriate behaviors or attitudes that guarantee longevity. Comparatively, a skilled based system with foreseeable career progression can offer the necessary commitment and ladder to capturing the next level of administration. External consultants bring the expertise, knowledge and information that is considered industry standard and simply proven to work, as a blueprint. The priorities are to observer and create solutions to fix issues and problems. Consultants support the executives and give them the backing and tools needed to effectively implement change. Alternatively, less number of advisors that foster team thinking and brainstorming to solve problems is an effective means to advance and develop healthier business practices and processes. The relation of the two managerial theories of change discussed in this writing covered goals, leadership, focus, process, rewards and consultants used to move a company forward. At the end of the day, once the decision has been made to conduct an appropriation of change in an organization, a leadership style must be adapted and a course must be plotted to achieve success. Discussed above are two very different methodologies that produce positive results, but are totally contrary. The key is to sustain by incorporating the two and with proper timing and delivery, merge the styles into lasting change and continuous improvement. The following organizations belong to the old world (Corporate America): Avon Products, Inc., is an

American producer and dispenser of beauty, household, and personal care products sold through representatives in over 140 countries across the world. As of 2013, Avon had annual net income of $51.7 billion worldwide. It is the fifth-largest beauty company and second largest direct selling enterprise in the world, with 6.4 million representatives. Amway is an American company using multi-level marketing techniques, that sells a variety of products, such as, jewelry, electronics, Nutrilite dietary supplements, water purifiers, air purifiers, insurance and cosmetics. At the end of December, 2012, Amway Inc., reported revenue of $11.3 billion. The following organizations belong to the new world online (Corporate America): (1) In 2012, Facebook was valued at $104 billion, and by January 2014 its market capitalization had risen to over $134 billion. At the end of January 2014, 1.23 billion users were active on the website every month, while on December 31, 2013, 945 million of this total were identified by the company as mobile users. (2) Groupon Inc., is an American company, a deal-of-the-day website that features discounted gift certificates usable at local or national companies. At the end of December 2013, Groupon was valued at $17 billion and 147 million users were active on the website every month. Groupon served more than 150 markets in North America and 100 markets in Europe, Asia and South America. Customers are now enjoying no time limit of services offered by the convenience of e-commerce business transactions. Several organizations are now actively participating on e-commerce business. On a global scale, online vendors do seize e-commerce profitable and cost efficient opportunities. The advent of e-commerce changed the online business orientation with five different types of e-commerce. Consequently, one is now familiar with (B2C) business-to-consumer e-commerce - describe company online that sells to shoppers, the standing example is Amazon.com. The next type is known as (B2B) business-to-business e-commerce – refer to company online that transacts business with each other, specifically with supplier; a popular example that comes to mind is ChemConnect.com. The third type is known as (C2C) consumer-to-consumer e-commerce – is the category where shopper conduct business with each other, an example that come to mind is ebay. The fourth type is called (P2P) peer-to-peer e-commerce - is the sort where people exchange music files with each while bypassing central web server. Finally, the mobile commerce - is the type where users can use wireless digital devices like blackberries to conduct business on the Internet. One thing abundantly clear is that the world witnessed the advent of (B2C) around March 1992; meanwhile, the notion of (B2C) was fully entrusted to the society through Netscape browser in year of 1994 and with the participation of Amazon.com in the year 1995. In addition, (B2C) started with the traditional sales of commodities however today (B2C) has evolved to offer varieties of commodities and services, for instance (B2C) now carries travel agencies like Travelocity.com, Expedia.com, and Priceline.com.

Moreover, (B2C) now offer online banking, automobile sales, life insurance sales, car insurance, real estate marketing, educational services, and other goods and services needed by the society. Conversely, the technical progression of Internet has minimized the expenses of (B2B), thus, small businesses are currently enjoying the privileges offer by the Internet. Financially (B2B) still supersedes and maintain the principal e-commerce functions. Governments have recognized the advantages of e-commerce. As a result, (G2C) government to consumer, (C2G) consumer to government, (G2B) government to business and (B2G) business to government sites have sprung up at the Federal, state, and local levels. One should be aware that (C2C) limelight began in 1995 the period eBay.com was inaugurated. (C2C) is the type of e-commerce where a consumer can actually act as both the seller and buyer; however, their business transaction materializes via an intermediary. Society is now conversant with the example of (C2C) such as online auction web site like (eBay.com, uBid.com, Overstock.com to name a few). The doctrine and the profitability of e-commerce have persuaded the Governments. Consequently, (G2C), (C2G), (G2B) and (B2G) sites have obviously manifested at the Federal, state, and local levels. For example, the U.S. government can boast of one of the prominent government e-business web sites that are normally controlled by the IRS to provide information, (G2C), and tax return filing (C2G). An astute observer is bound to recognize that the epoch of e-commerce (I) began in 1995 through 2001. Technological innovation contributed to the phenomenal growth of the e-commerce (I). This was a period when website was used to advertise company products and all the dot.com company's stock value that eventually collapse. Whereas the e-commerce (II) inauguration began in January 2001, hence the management of e-commerce (II) companies innovatively brought the successful campaign of order and rationality to the online industry this period transformed the online business because it depicted the reconstruction of online enterprise and aggrandizes the stock prices and value. The e-commerce (I) activated the following manifestations: (A) Technology-driven (B) Revenue growth emphasis (C) Venture capital financing (D) Ungoverned (E) Entrepreneurial (F) Disintermediation (G) Perfect markets (H) Pure online strategies (I) First mover advantages, whereas the e-commerce (II) proffer the (A) Business driven (B) Earnings and profit emphasis (C) Traditional financing (D) Stronger regulation and governance (E) Large traditional firms (F) Strengthening intermediaries (J) Imperfect markets, brands, network effects (H) Integrated. (I) Multi-channel (K) Bricks-and-click strategies (L) Strategic follower strength (M) Complimentary assets.

In my organization sometimes they do have frequent computer upgrades for example we recently went through what we call Network Implementation Project (NIP), this projects provides a complete re-design and upgrade of the Organization's Network Infrastructure. The organization Information Technology Department (ITD) crafted a schedule for the upgrade for the duration of five consecutive working days. Throughout this period ITD reconfigured the existing computers and printers onto a new wiring plant and network infrastructure. On scheduled days, data connectivity on specified departments are lost as data systems are moved over to the new network. This means that employees will not have access to email, the Internet, data files or networked applications. Employees were required to backup data and make necessary preparations to use manual processes until the network becomes available on the scheduled day. One thing is abundantly clear this network upgrade greatly enhances the performance and reliability of email, the Internet, data files or networked applications by adding increased capacity and eliminated redundancy. In modern companies this is one of several necessary steps in continuing effort to improve services and ability to serve better. The next paragraph will allow you to see the development and comparison of e-commerce category. Let us now look into the business model and how e-commerce revolutionized the business entities.

The following representations are the key elements of the business model: specifically, proposition, revenue model, market opportunity, competitive environment, competitive advantage, market strategy, organizational development, and management team. One would find that the representations of business model are noteworthy because they are paramount for stimulating booming business in any realm including e-commerce. The definition of value proposition is the enjoyment derivable when a company's product extended satisfaction to vast patrons. The e-commerce changed business orientation because shoppers have the advantage to personalize, normalize and customize their individual product, and they also have the convenience to purchase product on a twenty-four hours basis. In addition, e-commerce now allows merchandiser to enjoy low cost of advertisement, operation, and delivery and amass profitable revenue. The e-commerce model of revenue, advertising, subscription, marketing, transaction, fee, sales, and affiliate did transform business on a global scale. Netflix online company provides an outstanding example how e-commerce has transformed businesses and new company can now survive the rigor of the competitive atmosphere. Online product costs effectiveness, customer care, timeliness of product delivery, specification and customization of product are essential factors in online value proposition to consumers.

Furthermore, the innovations of e-commerce value propositions that transform business are derived from the society trend, whim and the state of the economy. For example, Amazon.com makes it probable for book lovers to shop for virtually any book in print from the ease of their residence or office, 24 hours a day, and to know immediately whether a book is in stock. Amazon primary value propositions are unparalleled selection and expediency. Organization should always strive to satisfy the desires of the consumer. E-commerce brought about the innovation of advertising revenue whereby a company that owns space on the websites obtains fees from vast online and traditional advertisers. This business novelty made it possible so that the higher the users of the websites the higher the amount the owner of the website can charge the advertisers. Consequently, e-commerce created the originality of online subscription revenue, thus Yahoo website offers its client vast amount of first-rate services and charges subscription fee of $5.95 a month for Yahoo! Plus, where the users enjoy the benefit of high-class online movies, brand new music videos, games, radio and massive storage email account. E-commerce implemented transaction revenue so the world of business online company like ebay.com get vast fee from seller whenever the individual sells an item. In addition, when customer procures a stock etrade.com collect transaction fee as online stockbroker. Sales revenue protocol is now in the field of online business, for instance, Amazon.com and half.com get revenue by selling online books, music, movies, videos and other product.

E-commerce produced the modernization of affiliate revenue hence such companies like MyPoint.com divert patrons to the partners companies and get recompense of great reward of revenue, fees and percentage of sales. In addition, epinion.com redirects businesses to associate companies and receive revenue. E-commerce brought about the market opportunity then new online company may now choose their own section of marketspace. For instance, new company have the chances to sell its products to vast numbers of small business firms who can only afford to spend $6 billion on computer software training even though they still yearn for low cost training resolution. One is now familiar with the competitive environment that spells out the thought process of finding out the existing competitors before new company enter the online marketspace. Society is now cognizance that the competitive advantage speaks about the privileges any firm is bringing to the online marketspace. Market strategy is all about the plan in store to advertise organization products or services to the target audience. Organizational development speaks about the kind of organization hierarchy available in the firm and the importance of their responsibilities to implement business plan. Management team should elucidate about the style of proficiency, expertise and education essential for the organizational leadership.

The web has enabled new business opportunities such as online multi-channels business enterprise, for example in my organization coworkers normally purchases their commodities from many channels via the telephone, email, internet, television and in store. We are all aware of coworkers who got the houses financed from low interest e-loan. Car insurance is compulsory in the State of Texas, one thing is certain, the cheapest premium are gotten from the e-insurance. The business models available in the e-commerce have revolutionized business on many forums. Thus, Internet being an equal opportunity technology has given easy access to competitor thereby making room for stronger competition. That being said, consumers now possess more buying powers because of the abundant information on the e-commerce therefore buyers can now disburse for inexpensive product from online merchandiser. Meanwhile, Internet is now creating quality, excellence, value, in order to brand online products and exacting premium prices. On the Web one should be expected to find brick and wall business like Wal-Mart or Sears. One thing is noteworthy, when a company craft efficient e-commerce business model the result would be, competitive advantage, productivity and higher income. Thus, one should be cognizance of the prominent e-commerce business models examples like Yahoo, eBay, IBM, Apple, and many others. Business model is popularly known and defined as an instrument through which organization produces revenue, profit and meet the needs of the variety of patrons. Whereas, some other sector define business models as the preplanned way of doing business and deliberately implemented to manifest profit in a marketplace. Meanwhile, in order to craft or improve on an e-commerce business model, business entities that indicate special resources would magnify the commodities value and insulate the company from competitors. Special resource might be e-commerce technology, brand name, durability of product, quality of commodities and services.

E-commerce model has changed the business because the function represents the potential revenue and non-revenue. Thus, the cogent monetary results included revenue that are increased because of the capacity growth and price differentiation, cost that are minimized because of the clever-way of reducing cost of good and operating cost, and minimization of asset carrying cost because of the management of the cost of working capital and/or fixed asset. However, the non-revenue that creates value may include a variety of visible or invisible results that may materialized because of the e-commerce implementation, for instance, products and services continuous quality improvement, short and quick product delivery schedule, state of the art customer satisfaction, world-wide extension of products services and information, availability and permanency of information. Ingredient such as value proposition model, value-added e-commerce offering supporting resources, revenue model, cost models and value creation could be utilized to craft a new e-commerce model and improve on current e-commerce models. Narrated ingredients are indispensable for developing well-organized e-commerce business models that will satisfy purchaser's aspiration, to cause higher business performance and to maintain organizational competitive edge via e-commerce.

Society knows that jobs are changing. They are

impacted by ongoing workplace changes, new technologies, and are rapidly becoming more knowledge based. To keep up will require continuous learning on employee part - an investment both on and off the job. Since training and development is a shared responsibility for both worker and the employer, organization commitment is to provide employee with lifelong learning opportunities. For example my organization offer intranet courses in Technology, Business Management, Safety and Technical training. Organization that implements this aspect of training can help workforce increase value, versatility, and career potential. Job performance and job satisfaction will improve. And, employee will be better able to achieve personal and career goals. Improving the performance of organization is a major part of employees' job. One should know that it is a difficult task to focus on in the midst of change, resource constraints, and uncertainty. Employee training can do a lot to identify the key business goals and challenges, and then prescribe specific learning activities to help achieve those goals. However, research on leading edge organizations and today's workforce reveals two things one should know. First, investing in the development of a professional, versatile workforce is the best defense against changing and uncertain times. And second, employees today know the work environment is changing and expect to be trained and kept current by their employer. Having said that, Let us look into the important factors that a manager needs to consider when construction an e-commerce site.

One thing remarkable is that website does contain basic web server software in order to respond to consumer requisition from HTML & XML pages. Arguably, constructing a website from the initial stage to the end is more appropriate in terms of ease and inexpensive, however, one should not rehabilitate the wheels of the old website. The organizational management should be cognizance that the best software to be considered for the development of website is popularly known as Apache. In addition, volume of consumers that populate e-commerce site could eventually crash the website. Thus, manager needs to procure IBM

WebSphere Commerce Professional Edition. Furthermore, manager should consider allowing the following IBM suite of tools to operate on IBM Pseries Unix-based computer servers: (1) WebSphere Application Server, (2) WebSphere Commerce, and (3) MQ Series Integrater. Cost benefit assumption would have one believe that when building a website it is inexpensive to keep one vendor such as IBM. Interestingly, the hardware that would be needed should amount to ten Web server Pentium 4.2 GHz computer processors and with ten processors the Website could handle more than 100, 000 concurrent users.

The World Wide Web is a group of Internet site all connected by search engines providing access to different information. Whereas, the Internet is a very large computer network made up of thousands of smaller network interacting to governmental, academic, business or entertainment. The World Wide Web is an Internet technology that permits people to access more than 6 billion plus web pages. Internet is a technology that integrates millions of individual computer into available network that enhances global communication between different demography and organizations. Let us now peruse the e-commerce security atmosphere and ways to curb the e-commerce security threats.

Amazingly, when people conduct business on the Internet they are confronted with the lack of security on credit card payment systems. Whenever there is business engagement between the purchaser and merchant on the Internet it is hard to know whether it is legitimate or not. One should now be aware that users are being exposed to lack of privacy and security. There is no way to decipher whether the merchant you are dealing with is authentic or criminal element located in the penitentiary. Shoppers could become a victim of credit card identity fraud or be using stolen credit cards. The merchant is liable when patrons cancel credit cards charges after the commodities have been delivered or the product downloaded from the Internet. The gravity of cybercrime is not fathomable at this moment however criminal activity perpetrated against e-commerce, online consumers and merchants are enormous. Thus, the people that occupy high echelon of e-commerce organization must find decisive resolutions. Society is now cognizance of the scope of security dilemma when doing business on the Internet, such as integrity of information illustrates that a perpetrator might sabotage consumer financial instrument and divulge classified dossier on the web site. Repudiation might occur hence consumer may deny charges or cancel payment on the products previously ordered. Authenticity security problem ensue mostly because of the difficulty to validate the true identity of the shoppers or merchants.

As far as confidentiality problems are concern, the Internet user classified information may be parading multiple web sites. Unauthorized individual or entities can peruse email correspondence. Privacy issues is another security problem such as propriety information communicated in course of online business engagement may be exchanged with unauthorized organization or criminal elements. Availability is also a security problem that entails web site closure and inaccessible. Phishing problem include a situation where criminal perpetrator deceptively collect confidential information on the Internet for financial enrichment. Hacking and cyber vandalism is a notorious dilemma of deliberately sabotaging a web site. Credit card fraud/theft is one of the nefarious activities that may prevent several consumers from e-commerce transactions. The problem of spoofing may ensue when criminal hackers disguise their identities; they normally transfer false e-mail addresses otherwise reroute a web link to a wrong address from the one requested and wrong address or site camouflaged as the intended destination. When it comes to the issues of service attack this problem entails a criminal hacker using the strategy of deluging and saturating a web site with redundant traffic in order to sabotage the network, impairing the web site, closing down the web site, and eventually spoiling consumer affinity. Sniffing is another dilemma that is tantamount to intercepting personal data from the network or publicizing the collected information on multiple web sites.

Inside job is a jeopardy that may confront e-commerce for instance employees who are privy to sensitive organizational information may eventually use them for nefarious activities or perhaps for financial enrichment. Poorly designed server and client software is another problem essentially when the software is too sophisticated it will eventually result in imperfection for a hacker to assail. Lastly, malicious code such as viruses, worms, Trojan horse and bot networks are serious problem to computer operation and reliability. Malicious code usually corrupts how the computer system operates and defaces the information created on the system. The universal caveat that seems to be commonly popular with several users is unawareness of data origination, sources and location. Thus, the problem of data impersonation needs to be absolutely resolved. In addition, confidence is also needed for the question of whether Internet phone calls will continue to function, email services will continue to operate and electronic commerce business will not be sabotaged by variety of hackers. One thing is certain for the remedy of technology mishap, consumers should develop plan for disruption caused by security problem if they would continue to conduct business on Internet. Society use fire escape and smoke detector the same wisdom will work well to forestall security problem and technological disaster. Thus, the following are best practices for consumers: device a backup copies for family pictures instead of uploading it only on the Internet, secure paper copies of monthly bank statement in the house this is good when online banking is not feasible.

Society is noted for being highly dependent on Web site network without being cognizance for Internet security failure. Meanwhile, several Internet hackers have exerted effort to sabotage it but thanks goodness Internet is still functioning. Web sites have been disrupted. E-mail has been visited with several Spam. Web sites has been congested and slowed down with computer worms. Fortunately, the Internet has been victorious over several attacks perpetrated against it Computer hackers are sophisticated criminals they are no longer using their basic home computer to assail;

alternatively they are now assaulting Internet Domain Name Server system to self-destruct. The duty of domain name server system is software that manipulates the Internet addressing system. Additionally, the function of domain name is to convert numeric IP addresses that look like 129.206.1.1 into a readable name format like MSNBC.com. Everybody is aware that the criminals have been assailing the local domain servers. The following narration is called spoofing or data identity theft: Hacker mode of operation is to cleverly ask smaller server fake questions combine with fictitious return address in order to reply bogus answer to several and different computers own by people and organization. This situation bears resemblance to a friend who wants to pull a prank hence he/she walks to the pizza parlor then order it anonymously and have it deliver to the friend's house.

Network operators are now apprehensive because the criminal element uses the domain name server software to magnify the intensity of the assaults. Hacker normally dispatch a fictitious question with a misleading return address to a company domain name server, the response is 64 times in maximization than the initial question. As a case in point, in 2003, notorious hacker emptied an attack at Microsoft's domain name servers, were successful in closing down the organization Web sites for three consecutive days. Puzzling as it may, computer relies on trustworthiness of any data input. Computer is like a baby that trusts everybody. Computers generally and honestly believe the return address that is approaching or what computer sees is what computer accepts. One knows that Internet was originally created to satisfy the need of bunch of trustworthy university professors. Although e-commerce is paramount for providing convenience for both consumers and merchants, whereas several consumers are now apprehensive about security, the concern for their personal dossier being jeopardize when buying commodities and services via the Internet. The vast presence and the competitive low cost of Internet have spawned creativity in e-commerce and its functions. Thereafter society glance several example of what the use e-commerce accomplish, to name few of them, online shopping, banking, telebanking, television teaching, distance education, online gambling, virtual casino, as well as Pay-Tv and video-on-demand services. Companies do benefit from the prospect produced by Internet-based e-commerce.

Current report stated that there has been several sabotage of a renowned Websites that involved theft of credit cards that belongs to vast customers. The major defect affecting e-commerce is security lapses. Patron's privacy is number one security criteria in the world of business transaction via the e-commerce. There is no consumer in this world that would like to participate in any business that would spread his or her personal information/dossier without obtaining permission. Thus, encryption technologies are now the solution that company/online merchandiser uses to preserve customer's privacy. In addition, with confidence many organizations are now depending on security measures provided by encryption algorithms and digital signature, they encourage security of email and electronic payment system. Another one of those solutions for e-commerce security anomalies includes software known as public key infrastructure (PKI). This PKI is a very effective tool that promotes tight security on all e-commerce business segments. Hacker's operations of spreading dangerous viruses are nemesis to e-commerce. They are noted for assailing networks or e-commerce sites thus they have the capability to close down the electronic services. There is power of defense behind the popular software known as the firewall; that is why several companies adopt the usage of this powerful software. Because of the firewall the security of online business transaction between vendors and consumers are adequate. Online companies are now enjoying the adequate protection from criminal oversight after the installations of systems such as Intrusion Detection System, Virtual Private Network and Information Retrieval System.

Proxy server use by several organizations, though it functions like firewall, this is another security protection that prevents any unlawful intrusion to the internal server even from the external server. Encryption provides technology solutions to the security problems such as converting text or data into cipher text so that interloper cannot read it thus the sender and receiver can peruse the communication. One is now confident of message integrity provided by encryption security and as a matter of fact this software adequately prevents an interloper from modifying confidential information. Thanks to the encryption software, society is now convince that repudiation of messages by online user is now history and can no longer be refuted. Encryption security is now able to depict the actual computer or identity of the perpetrator transferring the data, file and messages. Authentication and corroboration between the consumer and merchants is now feasible on the e-commerce. Encryption technology is now capable to protects individual confidentiality thus users can rest confident that their dossier are proprietary and cannot be perused by an authorized Internet interloper. The organization where I am employed has policy on Information Technology Security, as it relates to the use of the electronic technology resources. The company has established certain specific criteria for the use of the E: Mail function, including Instant Messaging.

In addition, criteria have been established for the use of the Internet and Intranet, Bulletin Boards and cellular phones, including camera and videophones. The use of Email, Inter and Intranet, Bulletin Boards and cellular phones should be limited to business use with some limited personal use allowed. The policy in my organization is clear which stated that the use of E: Mail for sensitive or secure communications should be limited since it is technologically possible for those with certain skills to access any messages that are sent. In addition, solicitation should not be made through E: Mail except to the extent that the solicitation for an organization sponsored or approved campaign, a holiday project or office event. Furthermore, the policy states that normally accepted business-related communication in informal, formal formats, informal informational, personal communications, including congratulatory and sympathy messages are permitted. Instant messaging is prohibited. The use of Bulletin Boards is restricted to purposes approved in writing by the management. Downloading, making use have or sending vulgar, harassing or offensive information or have sexually-oriented or explicit material, data or graphics is prohibited. The use of the picture, taking capabilities of computer or cellular phones is prohibited without the express written permission of the management. My organization may rightfully access and review employee usage of all company-owned electronic technology, including desktop computers, laptops, Blackberry's, telephones (including cellular phones) and so forth. Computer passwords are to be provided by the Information Systems Division of the Organization's Office or authorized IT personnel in conjunction with the Information Systems staff. Any violation of this policy may result in disciplinary action, up to and including termination of employment, and may also result in prosecution under the provision of any applicable law. The next paragraph will show us the role and process of payment system on e-commerce.

When a customer wants to acquire a product or service, he or she adds the item to the merchant's shopping cart. When the customer wants to pay for the items in the shopping cart, a secure tunnel through the Internet is created using Secure Sockets Layers (SSL). Using encryption, SSL safeguards the session during which credit card information will be conducted to the merchant and protects the information from impostors on the Internet. SSL does not validate either the merchant or the consumer. The transacting parties have to rely on one another. Once the merchant gets the consumer credit card information, the merchant software contacts a clearinghouse. A clearinghouse is a financial intermediary that validates credit cards and verifies account balances. The clearinghouse consults the issuing bank to verify the account information. Once verified, the issuing bank credits the account of the merchant at the merchant's bank (frequently this occurs at night in a batch process). The debit to the consumer account is conveyed to the consumer in a monthly statement.

The process of using digital payment systems or E-count is a revolution in itself hence the steps involve consumer setting up an account with E-count which is popularly funded by a credit debit, and smart cards. The account information is transported through the Web using the security protocol of SSL. After the verification of E-count account balance with the consumer's card issuing bank then shoppers can go on Web shopping spree wherever the credit card or digital payment is accepted. One should be aware that it is the responsibility of E-count to immediately debits the consumer's account and transfer the funds to the merchant. Monthly statements that represent debit on E-count are issue and convey to the purchasers by the consumer's card issuing bank. Shoppers can now enjoy the availability of transaction history provided online directly from E-count. Interestingly, coworkers are now participating in the pay-as-you-ride Smart Card payment system, if they work at an approved downtown location, drive to work and park in a downtown parking lot, or relocate to an approved downtown work location. The Smart Card payment system will provide employees with one daily roundtrip from Metro Park and Ride Lots to approved downtown facilities.

The agreeable solution to the Internet irregularity seems to result in the preponderance of the digital credit card payment systems. Online merchants seems to have rest of minds because of digit credit card payment that now helps to eliminate the problems of no authentication, cancellation of charges, credit card fraud, and on the other hand, the buyers are now confident to use their credit cards. Informal online observer knows that the digital checking payment system is another form of payment system that protects buyers' privacy. There are many attributes allocated to digital checking payment systems, such as faster than traditional checking account, cost effective than credit cards, privacy and prevent consumers information on Web.

The most significant tasks of a digital wallet are: (1) provision of trustworthy payment method from the online shopper to the vendor, (2) validate the authenticity of the online shopper via the use of digital signatures, (3) confidential financial information of consumer are compile and convey to the online merchant. Whereas, the major advantages of digital wallets are: (1) online shopper enjoy simplicity and cheap transaction costs because order requisition is so prompt (2) minimization of fraud and stolen credit cards (3) transaction costs effectiveness, market expansion and branding prospect, (4) effortless customer retention, and (5) smoother conversion of visitors into buyers. Digital cash permit online purchaser to easily and securely make payment to organization or online peers for goods under the amount of $200.

An online stored value system is a novelty that allows websites patrons to make cursory bill payment to online vendors from the monetary and vital information loaded in an online account. However, online stored value system may only functions after download of a digital wallet, conversely, other stored value only need sign up to convey money from web site stored value account. Digital accumulating balance systems normally permit customers to buy products on the Internet thus aggrandizing monthly bill payment, however, consumer are not allowed to make installment payment but they must use their checking or credit card account to make full payment. The accumulating balance systems are normally use by consumer to buy products such as intellectual property, newspaper articles, music tracks or chapter of books.

Digital credit card payment systems advantages includes the propensity to eradicate the anomalies of lack of authentication, customer cancellation of payment, the notorious credit card fraud, identity theft, transaction cost cutting, and producing client confidence to purchase online with credit card. Apparently, digital credit card no longer allows the disclosure of consumer financial information on the multiple websites. The digital checking payment system arrived from the framework of long established checking account and banking enterprises. There are many benefits associated with digital checking payment system for instance online buyer are not oblige to indicate their bank account information to other party when paying money for the auction, consumers are now free from the fear of uploading significant financial information on the Internet, digital checking payment system are cheaper than credit card for the benefit of online companies, and digital checking payment system are quicker than paper checks provided by the banks. The long-established payment systems such as cash, check, credit and debit cards will not work in the digital arena of Internet. As people maximize buying potential on websites the side effect of cash, check, credit, and debit cards might become more obvious. Consequently, organization have now innovated series of digital payment systems to satisfy the demand of the online consumer and merchant. The next paragraph will show us the functions of e-commerce marketing and branding line of attack.

One thing that is noteworthy about B2C and B2B e-Commerce it possesses different kinds of operation, for instance, B2C e-Commerce marketing system are directed towards individual purchaser that normally make the buying decision. On the other hand, B2B e-Commerce marketing systems are directed towards group decision makers. The brand of a product is responsible for making the merchandise stands out incomparable in the conscience of the shopper; therefore, online merchant should strategize on product quality, reliability, consistency and specialty. A good entrepreneur would build on consumer trust, affection, loyalty and thought process for their product. In addition, astute marketers should differentiate their products and communicate this difference substantially in the marketspace in order to obtain competitive advantage over the competitors. The far-reaching brand strategy involves segmenting the market, targeting different market segments with differentiated products, and positioning products to appeal to the needs of segment customers. For instance, Netflix an Online organization started building its brand by marketing the company services with the strategy of procuring pay-for-performance banner. In addition, customers can take the advantage of free self-addressed stamped mailer for postal returns. In addition, Netflix e-commerce site offers product free trial period and won vast numbers of consumers. Accordingly, the infamous website of Yahoo, MSN, and AOL propagated Netflix advertisement.

Brand equity is the estimated value of the premium customers are willing to pay for using a branded product when compared to unbranded competitors. Consumers are willing to pay more for branded products in part because they reduce consumers' search and decision-making costs. The ability of brands to attain brand equity also provides incentive for firms to build products that serve customer needs better than other products. Moreover, brands also lower customer acquisition cost and increases customer retention. Although some forecasted that the Web would lead to frictionless commerce and the expiration of marketing based on brands, recent research has publicized that brands are in public eye on the Web and that consumers are still willing to pay price premiums for products and services they observe and differentiate. Society saw the advent of cost efficient and vast accessibility of the Internet and how it brought into focus a massive ingenuity in electronic commerce and its applications. Various organizations have begun exploiting the opportunities made available by Internet-based e-commerce, and many more are anticipated to follow. Exemplary applications include online shopping, telebanking and Internet banking, television-teaching and distance education, online gambling, and virtual casinos, including Pay-Tv and video-on-demand services. Let us now look into marketing and communication online.

The online marketing communication is the system and practices that online entrepreneur employ to stimulate shopper's interest in their products and advertise their brand. Thus, as online entrepreneur want to attract potential purchaser to the Web site therefore marketers need to be knowledgeable about the online marketing procedures. Conversely, the obvious growing channel in consumer marketing is the multi-channel shopper. As matter of fact the lower amounts of expenses incurs from the cost of doing business are major parts of the benefit of marketing, communicating and advertising online. Thus as an example, the cost per purchase for TV was $17, while the cost per purchase for online advertising was $11. In addition to sales, there are vast benefits and advantages of marketing and communicating online, which includes progressive brand knowledge of company products. One thing is very important; brand equity would eventually produce sales revenue and profitability. The online merchant also have the benefit to be able to measure precisely the exact amount revenue generated by a definite banners or e-mail messages sent to prospective customers. Although major benefits and advantages of marketing depends online marketing inputs, however, online merchants can maximize their campaign after viewing the effectiveness of online marketing.

The finding is now available that a low click-through rate does positively convey the advertisement impact on the consumers because just reading the advertisement is enough to enlist interest even when users fails to directly respond by clicking. Online advertising is now infamous for maximizing brand vast familiarity, understanding, discernment, and consumer propensity to procure. Generally speaking everybody is cost conscious. It is interesting to note that when one compares the cost between traditional mass media marketing and online marketing communications the Web is less costly. What a great benefit, in that accurate revenue is known when online merchant send a specific banners or certain e-mail messages to a potential client.

There are many benefits of marketing and communication; on a global scale it provides people about the detail awareness of online vendors, available products, price tags, quality, and durability. In addition, shoppers can now enjoy freedom of choice; selection, expression and consumers can spend their money for cost efficient product. The reward of marketing and communication are beneficial to marketers and consumers. E-commerce can now boast of reward attributable to vast consumer attraction, buyer targeting, data mining, consumer behavior trail, standardized messages, bilateral communication between marketers and consumers, and rapport between punters and customer services and because of this growing Internet usage among the general public, the Internet has already been exerting a extensive impact on our society in general, as well as on imperative disciplines and practices such as communications, marketing, and advertising.

Internet is a new interaction system therefore there is many potential research opportunities to be conducted in the areas of communication, marketing, and advertising. By and large, Internet has stimulated several research theme and prospects to date. Society now understands that the Internet is a proper medium to manage online business for profit, marketing, and advertisement. In 1994, the society saw the reward of the advertisement contract between Hotwire and the AT&T and the commencement of e-commerce in AOL. The global communities have been adequately apprised of how novel and indispensable the Internet is, for example, in the realms of education, communication, marketing and advertising. Let us now peruse Internet marketing technologies.

Internet marketing technologies goal is to dispense guidance, resources, and services subsequently the users need to seize the advantage of and opportunities of today and tomorrow. Internet and ordinary marketing has general resemblance because their main purpose is to accumulate vast consumers in order that the company can maximize its revenue, however, Internet marketing has disparity from ordinary marketing. Internet marketing is also very different from ordinary marketing because Internet marketing technologies now has market-space instead of market place. The Internet marketing technologies is now allowing marketing communication to be conducted at home, work and on a mobile dimension; sky is now the limit of Internet marketing. Internet marketing technologies brought about market-space instead of traditional market place, which is now on a global village. The advent of Internet marketing technologies has spawned convenience at the same time minimizing shopping costs.

Internet marketing interaction is on a global reach thus the world acclimatizes to global customer service. The doctrine of marketing is now reaching hundreds of millions of consumers. The expenses of disseminating the veracity of marketing and receiving response from shopper is minimized the reason being there is one universal standard for Internet. The e-commerce technological aspect of commodities and services personalization and customization for the benefit of customer thus maximizes the ability of marketer to craft brands. The luxury of video, audio and text does accompany the Internet marketing creed thus it can be combined to bring about richness in consuming experience. The introduction of Internet marketing is allowing consumers to chat thus becoming a co-manufacture of the commodities and services offered for sale. Merchandisers are now busy collecting the consumer financial information and online behavior for marketing research analysis. In order to better serve consumers, Internet marketing technology allows data mining for analysis of consumer data statistics for marketing research.

On balance, the Internet has had three very broad impacts on marketing. The Internet, as a communications medium, has widened the scope of marketing communications-in the sense of the number of people who can be simply reached. Second, the Internet has maximized the richness of marketing communications by joining text, video, and audio content into rich messages. Third, the Internet has abundantly increased the information intensity of the marketplace by providing marketers (and customers) with unequaled fine-grained, detailed real-time information about customers as they transact in the marketplace. Arguably, the Web is richer as a medium than even television or video because of the intricacy of messages available, the enormous content accessible on a wide range of subjects, and the capability of users to interactively control the experience. We have seen how Internet and e-commerce has given vast freedom to the consumer and merchant. This technology has made it possible for global patrons to use their finances to procure variety of commodities. One is now familiar with how Internet has spawned the twenty-four hours liberty to the consumers to procure amenities thus contributing to good standard of living. Global society enjoys no limit of the products and services offered by the convenience of e-commerce business transactions and time is no longer the issue. Several organizations are now actively participating in e-commerce business and enjoying the capitalism. On a global scale, online vendors do seize e-commerce profitable and cost efficient opportunities.

Toyota Motor Corporation was first established in 1937 as a separated company from Toyota Automobile Loom works was then headed by Sakichi Toyoda, the king of investors. Toyota Motor Corporation was then founded by Kiichiro Toyoda, Sakichi's son. It has since blossomed into the leader it is today. The giant automaker faced its one and only strike in 1950. This event, however, supplied Toyota an important philosophy, giving it the labor and management system which helped Toyota to gain mutual growth and success in both domestic and overseas markets. Today, this philosophy is very important to the structure of Toyota. Since Toyota was founded in 1937, Toyota Motor Corporation has contributed to the development of the automobile industry and society by providing people with quality vehicles. Toyota Motor Corporation manufactures automobiles in 25 countries and regions all over the world. Today, its vehicles are sold in more 160 nations worldwide under the brand names of Toyota, Lexus, Daihatsu, and Hino, manufacturing small cars to luxury sedans, full sized pickup trucks, and crossover vehicles. The recent significant success of Toyota is in the fiscal year ended March 31, 2002 in which Toyota Motor Corporation and its overseas subsidiaries sold 5.54 million passengers cars, trucks, and busses around the world. The helps position Toyota Motor Corporation as the world's number three in the term of automobiles sold, staying behind General Motor and Ford, respectively.

Today, there are varying brands of vehicles available for drivers to choose. Some countries which are unable to produce automobiles in the past now produce cars. This is because many countries can now afford the technologies were expensive in the past, but have lower price in these days. This factor persuades many countries to go into car producing industry. The world's automobile market is now very competitive. The main competitors of Toyota are

General Motor and Ford who tie in the ranking of number one and two in the term of net sale and unit sale.

Flexible manpower line means preparing a production line so that it can meet changing production requirements with any number of workers without lowering productivity. In contrast, a fixed manpower line is one that always requires a fixed number of workers. No upward or downward adjustment can be made in it to meet changes in production demand. The five S's are the corresponding Japanese and English terms of Seiri-Sifting, Seiton-Sorting, Seiso-Sweeping, and Seiketsu-Spick and Span. Collectively they mean the maintenance of an orderly, clean and efficient working environment. Just in time, is one of the two main pillars of the Toyota Production system. It refers to the ability of production lines to be stopped in the event of such problems as equipment malfunctions, quality problems or work being late either using machines which have the ability to sense abnormalities or using worker who push a line stop button. This prevents passing on defects. Reoccurrence prevention becomes simpler as abnormalities become more obvious making it possible to build in quality at the production process. At the same time, since defects are prevented automatically, inspectors become unnecessary, which in turn results in significant labor savings. Just in time refers to the manufacturing and conveyance of only what is needed, in the amount needed. This enhances efficiency and enables quick responses to change.

Kanban, this is a small signboard that is the key control tool for just in time production. Kanban serves instruction for production and conveyance, a tool for visual control, to check against over production, to detect irregular processing speeds, and a tool to perform kaizen. Production instruction kanban is used to order the start of production at each production job site. Production lead time refers to the time it takes to provide one product from acceptance of order to shipment. It is defined as follows, production lead time = A + B +CA: from order reception to beginning of work. B: from beginning of work on raw materials to completing product (processing + non processing time). C: from completion of first to last piece of one unit of conveyance.

Set up time is divided into three elements as follows: 1. off line set up, time during which machine is not stopped. 2. on line set up, time during which machine is stopped. 3. Adjustment time, time after set up finished that machine is stopped to obtain necessary quality levels or resolve problems. Set up time is the time it takes to change over from the production of one product to another, from the instant that the processing of the last component of one type is finished, to the production of the first food sample of the next type of component. It includes all the time needed for changeover of the dies, cutting tools, etc... Set up time = online set up time + adjustment time.

Toyota's production system improved in the late 1950's, establishing the "Toyota Production System." This system became the major factor in the reduction of inventories and defect in the plants of Toyota and its suppliers. It also underpinned all of Toyota's operations across the world. It launches its first small cars in 1947. The operation outside Japan started in 1959 in Brazil and continued with growing network of foreign plants. Toyota production System is the manufacturing system developed by Toyota which pursues optimum streamlining throughout the entire system through the elimination of Muda non value added and aims to build quality in at the manufacturing process while recognizing the principle of cost reduction. It also includes all the accompanying technology necessary to accomplish those aims. The two main sub systems supporting the Toyota production system are just in time.

Partnerships of suppliers and purchasers that remove waste and drive down costs for mutual benefits. The goals of just in time partnerships, is to eliminate unnecessary activities, in plant inventory, in transit inventory and poor supplier. Just in time partnerships is leading organization view suppliers as extensions of their own organizations and expect suppliers to be fully committed to improvement. They make sure that the shipment is shipped in the time that it should arrive to the company. They also make sure that the quantities of the shipment are correct and then once everything is in place they make sure that the buyers are satisfied. Every step in making Toyotas, from development to production, consists of joint work with suppliers. As you can see, Toyota plays an important role in the world's automobile market, placing as the world's third automaker in the term of net sale and unit sale. This is because Toyota has efficient strategies and ways for coping with cultural barriers. It also looks ahead in the future aiming to be the best automobile in automaker industry. This innovative concept and strategy will help Toyota to produce the vehicles that make people proud of. It is not surprised to learn if Toyota cars are known as the automobiles of the future.

We are cognizance of the victorious integration of the scientific management in the automobile industries and the administration of the workforce after the conversion. We have perused the automobile industry organization system before the transformation. The results of this research provide some fascinating insights into how automobile industries were profoundly transformed during the first half of the twentieth century. A casual observer is now acclimated with the system of management in the automobile industry and their nature before, during, and after the advent of the scientific management. Overall, one can now see how the empirical thought processes brought modernization into the global organizations.

The word automobile, derived from the Latin words, which meant self-moving and given to us by the French, represents one of the most quintessential industrial products that man has produced since the invention of the wheel. The automobile industry has become the bedrock of our life and most of the global economy. In fact, the net earnings of the industry have become so huge, that metaphorically, it could circle the planet earth a thousand times over. The industry produces different types of automotive products such as trucks, buses, cars, ambulances, armored cars and automobile parts and the automobile was responsible for the liberty of people to be able to travel from coast to coast which led to the urbanization and modernization of the cities. The remainder of this passage will consider the significant changes and effects of the management theory on the automobile industry. The results of this research provide some fascinating insights into how automobile industries were profoundly transformed during the first half of the twentieth century. A casual observer is now acclimated with the system of management in the automobile industry and their nature before, during, and after the advent of the scientific management.

The history of the automobile industry propagates that the automobile was actually invented by several individuals who contributed solid knowledge to the innovation. Accordingly, the other findings include a notation that the 1890s was also the period when commercial automobile production in U.S. was in full swing. Technology availability brought into focus new ideals, firms and industries and their development consequently led to managerial systems that governed the workforce of the automobile and other industries. Among the many names that come to mind on the exhaustive list of automotive pioneers, are the infamous Henry Ford and his 1903 Ford Motor Company, Ransom Eli and his 1897 Olds Motor Company, David D. Buick and his 1903 Buick Motor Car Company, William Durant and his 1903 General Motors and finally Louis Chevrolet who bought General Motors in 1905. In the nineteenth century, industrial systems were notorious for lack of motivation, planning, performance evaluation, accountability, and management techniques. Furthermore, by the end of the nineteenth century, though, increased competition, novel technologies, pressures from government and labor, and a growing consciousness of the prospective of the industry had stimulated a widespread search for improved organization and management.

Frederick W. Taylor was the father and the proponent for the advancement of scientific management thought. Industries in USA had already witnessed conversion from sole proprietor, manager-owner firms to large-scale firms and corporations. Taylor preached about the integrity of scientific management and won the approval of several industries including the automobile industry. He was a pragmatist who gave all the industries including automobile industry the creativity, business policy, management viewpoint, logistic competence, business, and organization prudence. Accordingly, industries in United States could boast of market growth and increasing technology, while on the other hand there was labor unrest and a severe deficiency in management skills. For-profit organizations, which needed to meet the goals, objectives, customers' needs, market share, and the internal and external stakeholders' needs would now benefit from this type of progression. Goals and output would now be met at lower costs and half the time. Therefore, industry in America became fertile ground from which knowledge of manufacturing and marketing methodologies could be gained. To provide a remedy, Taylor advanced the solution of enhanced productivity that affected all industries including automobile industries. For example, several industries including the automobile industry enjoyed the innovation of efficiency and planning department to discharge the duties that were vital; staff specialists to bring proficiency to the industry; time study to allocate benchmarks for production and control; apparatus layout and design; and benchmarks of tools and methods.

As early as the 1920s, scientific management innovatively brought the successful campaign of order and rationality to the automobile industry. It could be seen that because of this principle, management provided adequate supervisory oversight on the work of the subordinates; similarly they provided planning, performance evaluation, accountability, and employee motivation. Moreover, because of the scientific management the automobile industry acclimated to the tenets of management thereafter, there was substance in planning, specialization of function, and formal relationship. Scientific management influenced the automobile industry via the principles of timeliness, effectiveness, better performance, supervision and assets manipulation. Taylor's principles that were based on science allowed automobile industries and others to enjoy collaboration, teamwork and agreement. The thought process of the scientific management movement cried out for workforce salary boost, industrial harmony, and abundant productivity. It later created the publicity of management, industrial education, and service to citizens and enhanced productivity.

The renowned Frederick W. Taylor, as people knew from history, was categorized as the authentic father of Scientific Management. Taylor scientifically studied work methods because he yearned to simplify work processes, better performance and increase productivity. He used scientific and empirical methods to create work standards. His uphill struggle eventually paid off and he cleverly gave us management benchmarks with which to work. Taylor triumphed by extending scientific management to future organizations. Similarly, Henri Fayol concocted other managerial functions such as planning, organizing, staffing, monitoring and controlling; Lillian Moller Gilbreth invented motion studies, psychology, fatigue, morale, monotony and micro-motion systems; and Mary Parker Follett and Chester Barnard discovered psychosocial and humanistic theories. Eventually, in the 1930s management was duly accepted as a profession.

Scientific management had a simple beginning from Midvale Steel Company in 1878, where Taylor saw employees who deliberately reduced production because of their fear of unemployment. However, Taylor innovatively discovered methods of timing workers to ascertain the timeliness of job completion. There are major achievements attributed to the management profession as a result the businesses has advanced with continuous improvement on efficiency, governance and productivity. The management profession involves daily interaction with different types of human behavior that may be overwhelmingly intricate to decipher. The job requirement of managers now includes the ability to understand, retain and motivate employees. Thus, managers are responsible for helping organizations to capitalize and maximize organizational resources (Stanley, 2004, November). One would think that these common business practices like inventory management, quality inspection, error tolerable rate, policies, procedures, and advertisement would also be available in the automobile industry.

Carl Barth successfully implemented the principles of scientific management at Franklin Motor Car Company because the organization wanted to maximize its production capacity. Similarly, he also implemented a successful management principle in the Franklin Motor Car Company and the company saw high productivity, reduced turnover and profitability. Correspondingly, Ford was admired for using the effective methods of the moving assembling line, and division of labor, and converted to moving belt magnetos, which reduced assembly time from twenty-nine minutes to five minutes. One should be able to enlist employees in aggregate decision-making process to the degree that the workers would recognize his/her involvement. The end result could well be higher productivity, performance, satisfaction, motivation and commitments. Consequently, automobile industries approved Taylor principles of cost accounting, scheduling, organizing parts, incentive, motivation and free movement of automobile materials. Much more could be said about the benefit attributed to the advent of logistics, production control, shop floor, and time studies to monitor productivity.

Ford's prosperity aggrandizement encouraged and invited other automobile manufacturers to implement the root of Ford Motor Company success story. There were several imitators of Ford's technical innovation, assembly lines, mass production, interchangeable parts and most of all, the scientific management. Further-more, when Taylor passed away his colleagues of the same persuasion successfully implemented scientific management into 181 American factories. As a case in point, automobile industries and other industries varied the lighting of the workplace to encourage maximum productivity from the employees. Similarly, they installed music systems, favorable temperatures, incentive programs, and flexible work hours and enhanced work environment to stimulate employee productivity. In addition, research has been conducted for several time periods to find out the strategies to curtail turnover, retain employees and increase their levels of production. People have discovered that all employers need to increase production and lower turnover is employee motivation and acknowledgement. When an organization acknowledges its employees it serves two purposes; it creates an incentive to meet company goals and it satisfies employees. The organization needs to continue as a going concern or exist, in order to meet this goal they need to keep their best employees around and satisfied. When these needs are met, organization operations would flow efficiently, company goals and manufacturer numbers would be met and everything else would fall into place accordingly.

The general assumption would admit that automobile industries had employees schedule, involvement, training, turnover, defect, and employees were probably reprimanded for tardiness. Thus, the management function of automobile industries is rooted and grounded on the foundation of scientific management. Moreover, company management is crucial, as a consequence, all organization rely on leaders who are supportive of organizational objectives. Meanwhile, in order to administer the job requirement of managing, these five traditional managerial functions that a manager must be proficient in using are planning, organizing, staffing, monitoring and controlling.

The system at the automobile industry included unplanned organization, decentralized management, informal relations between organization and workforce. Furthermore, industrial system at automobile company was characterized as lack of job requirement of the applicant, experience, mentor, job description, accountability and assignment. Conversely, by the nineteenth century, the pressures started coming from the government regulation, labor, people, similarly from competition, new technologies and the society were expecting the ideal system from the industry. Consequently, this led to several active participants in the establishment of management benchmarks; meanwhile, these are the major early management accomplishments: Division of work, proper authority, orderly workplace, chain of command, discipline and respect, fair treatment and equity, mode of payment in wages, planned work-force and stability, unity of direction and command, esprit de corps, unity and harmony.

Automobile industries benefited from Taylor principles that included the notions such as how to schedule productions, cost accounting, organizing material that allowed managers to know the logistics of records, the production control, the awareness of shop floor, time studies to show the capabilities of each employees, piece rate system to teach employees to obey instruction and to measure how employees are being compliant with the instructions. Moreover, Taylor was an innovator that brought substantive revision to the automobile shop management systems, via time study; he brought benefit such as scientific selection of the applicant, trained workforce and division of labor. Furthermore, the principle became a big success so Henri fayol mentioned its application to the whole organization not only the factory.

One hundred and eighty one automobile industries were inculcated with the principles of scientific management with positive development and it proved the critics to be wrong. It is admitted that Taylor concepts advocated for skilled workers that pays attention on their main specialties. In summary: (1) The authority of the first line-supervisor curtailed and transferred to the managers (2) eradication of delay, (3) higher productivity, (4) employees decisions were objective, (5) structured work assignments, (6) salary increase, (7) incentive, (8) increased skills and as the improved scheduling and accounting was implemented, it nearly eliminated the laborers because new technology of material handling machine appeared in the workplace (Nelson, 1999; Wren, 2005; Thomson, 2006). The organized labor eventually accepted the principle of the scientific management. Furthermore, the union leaders amicably discovered that it is more profitable for them to comply with the concept and principle delineated by Taylor. Union leaders also noted that the entire standard favors the workforce collective bargaining process and curtails the management absolute power. However, Ford Motor

Company were compliant with Taylor injunction, hence the managers received more formal authority; production was adequately managed and monitored, they eradicated unproductive time, skilled workers focused on their main specialties.

The general assumption would concur that automobile industries had employees schedule, involvement, training, turnover, defect, and employees were probably reprimanded for tardiness. Thus, the management function of automobile industries is rooted and grounded on the foundation of scientific management. Moreover, company management is crucial, as a consequence, all organization rely on leaders who are supportive of organizational objectives. Meanwhile, in order to administer the job requirement of managing, these five traditional managerial functions that a manager must be proficient in using are planning, organizing, staffing, monitoring and controlling.

The crowns that proficient managers wear to workplace are several. This was probably true in automobile industries and other industries. Work environment is overwhelmingly difficult; as a result, managers must have the capability of multi-tasking with his/her function according to company project. It is the responsibility of managers to perform duties and succeed, therefore, managers must be proficient in the following activities "(1) monitor, (2) figurehead, (3) leader, (4) liaison, (5) disseminator, (6) resource allocation, (7) spokesperson, (8) architect of change, (9) entrepreneur, and (10) negotiator.

Concern in the nineteenth century was expressed about the issue of automobile industrial system. The system at the automobile industry included unplanned organization, decentralized management, informal relations between organization and workforce. Furthermore, industrial system was characterized as lack of job requirement of the applicant, employees, lack of job description and assignment. Conversely, by the nineteenth century, the pressures started coming from the government regulation, labor, people, similarly from competition, new technologies and the society were expecting the ideal system from the industry. There were several active participants in the establishment of management benchmarks; meanwhile, these are the major early management accomplishments: Division of work, formal authority, orderly workplace, chain of command, discipline and respect, fair treatment and equity, mode of payment in wages, planned work-force and stability, unity of direction and command, esprit de corps, unity and harmony.

Automobile industries benefited from Taylor principles that included the notions such as how to schedule productions, cost accounting, organizing material that allowed managers to know the logistics of records, the production control, the awareness of shop floor, time studies to show the capabilities of each employees, piece rate system to teach employees to obey instruction and to measure how employees are being compliant with the instructions. Moreover, Taylor was an innovator that brought substantive revision to the automobile shop management systems, via time study; he brought benefit such as scientific selection of the applicant, trained workforce and division of labor. Furthermore, the principle became a big success so Henri fayol mentioned its application to the whole organization not only the factory.

One hundred and eighty one automobile industries were inculcated with the principles of scientific management with positive development and it proved the critics to be wrong. It is admitted that Taylor concepts advocated for skilled workers that pays attention on their main specialties. In summary: (1) The authority of the first line-supervisor curtailed and transferred to the managers (2) eradication of delay (3) higher productivity (4) employees decisions were based on personal judgment (5) structured work assignments (6) salary increase (7) increased skills (8) and as the improved scheduling and accounting was implemented, it nearly eliminated the laborers job because new technology of material handling machine appeared in the industry.

Management cannot assume employees are happy and satisfied because they produce well and come to work every day. Having an open door policy established at least once a week to discuss issues or just have a conversation would make such a positive difference in the work environment. This will allow management to know their employees at a more personal level and employees will feel comfortable talking because there is an assigned day for discussions instead of feeling like intruders on their boss's time. The organized labor eventually accepted the principle of the scientific management. Furthermore, the union leaders amicably discovered that it is more profitable for them to comply with the concept and principle delineated by Taylor. After the entire standard favors the employees' collective bargaining process and curtails the management absolute power. However, Ford Motor Company were compliant with Taylor injunction, hence the managers received more formal authority; production was adequately managed and monitored, they eradicated unproductive time, skilled workers focused on their main specialties.

Ford Motor Company implemented the strategies of scientific management, which influenced even the design of the machine operations, which as a consequence, its popularity became favorably magnified. Society saw abundant availability of vehicles in the market during the mid-1920s. To increase sales, the automobile industry directed its marketing schemes on two-car families. In order to ease quick purchase the industry created easy financing through which families bought 75% cars on installment payment. Automobile industries saw the benefit of efficiency and performance and the following are the fulfillment of the great recompense of reward: (1) higher profit margins, (2) amplified sales, (3) bigger market share, (4) larger net income, (5) lesser costs, (6) superior asset utilization, (7) improved innovation, and (8) less accidents.

There was a high ownership of Ford cars through easy financing; they had the advantage of technological machinery, mechanical devices, faster production, novel manufacturing systems, mass production, good scheduling systems, production management, salary incentives and division of labor. In order to attract supportive human resources and reduce turnover, Ford started paying higher salaries to unskilled workers. During the first half of the twentieth century Henry Ford was popularly known for his ingenious automobiles manufacturing systems. Similarly, society was aware of the employees' financial empowerment. Consequently, Ford stated that untrained, inexperienced workers could earn higher wages in his company within a few days.

The business society knew that Ford inventions was very supportive of the principle of the scientific management and it several associates. The component and design of Ford Motor Company's machine operation adhered to the principles of Taylor's scientific management. The manager function at Ford saw job enlargement, they had a rigid manufacturing planning, downtime was eliminated, skilled workers were focus and specialized, one would notice that they followed Taylor injunction. The unskilled employees were permitted to work overtime and they were highly paid. Ford's phenomenal escalation in the decade after 1907 forced other manufacturers to adjust to focus on market niches, or to go out of business, several others, including Dodge (as cited in Ford's early partner). General Motors (GM) started imitating Ford systems and scientific management, thus, by 1920's this translated GM into industrial giant in assembly techniques and industrial engineering. GM managers accepted personnel management into their policy and were involve in the development of welfare capitalism. The global society saw Ford Motor Company outstanding technical prowess, accomplishments and increased salaries allocated to the employees; hence, world organizations were won over by the principle of scientific management.

The aftermath of the twentieth century the automobile industry made changes that can never be erased, for example the automobile industry brought the following "...human geography--of race, class, and power--is the unique product of the automobile age. And it's built and natural environments are also the product and by-product of the car itself. At the dawn of a new century, amidst celebrations of the advent of the new, revolutionary technology of the computer and the internet (dubbed the electronic superhighway); we are still a nation of cars, of highways, of sprawl, of industrial decentralization. We still reside in the automobile nation. Let us now look into the early attempts to develop business efficiency.

Taylor configured work design that he spawned through the concept of time and motion technique. He was persuaded that the time and motion systems would stimulate higher productivity and efficiency for a company and increase salary for the employees. In addition, he advocated that the management responsibilities to motivate workforce in order for them to avoid negligence of duty or soldiering. Further, he said responsibility of a company is to rehabilitate and design work environment, peripherals and standard. He also propounded that when an organization becomes a paragon of efficiency there should be abundant productivity then the aggrandizement of opulence would ensued and the nemesis of liquidation will be eradicated. The next paragraph will allow you to see the development of human resource management.

The human resources management was develop as a reaction to disgruntled employees, governmental law and cultural inclination. However, progressive company normally would satisfy their workforce because when employees are motivated there will be an increase in performance, net income and productivity. Conversely, employee absenteeism, turnover, lack of prior experience and skills were the nemesis that caused the development of human resources management. Consequently, business thinkers were then successful to invent HR for the responsibilities of employee selection, training, incentive, benefit and compensation. Let us now focus on the development of organizational theory. Henri Fayol gave all industries including automobile industries the privileges of academic recommendations for the management, planning, organizing, commands coordination and control. Max Weber fed all industries including automobile industries the nourishment of how to employ an applicant based on qualification, job requirement and policies. The next paragraph will allow you to see the Hawthorne Studies.

The Hawthorne plant research proved that

combination of incentive program and the interpersonal skill that supervisor uses would increase employees' satisfaction and performance. Thus, manager or leader must be proficient in good rapport, people skills, understanding and attentiveness. Similarly, Hawthorne research basically advocated for the management to become the caretaker of employees not production, instead of organization hierarchy focus employee betterment, motivate and increase financial incentives. Let us look into the development of organizational theory. Follett brought about the concept of humankind while Gestalt talked about psychology system of organizational theory, however, they discussed about teamwork, unity, harmony and commonality among corporate members. The next paragraph will allow you to see the evolution of people and organizational development.

The organizational development came out in two ways, first of all, as people started the questionnaire about who and how to make decisions, characteristics of groups, social norms, leadership and how to satisfy employees. They were known as human relation, this committee stressed that the companies should adopt the concepts of management that favors socialization, job enlargement, eradication of organization structure, focused on flat structure, and group participation in management.

Accordingly, the period after 1920s saw new industrial system victoriously compliant with the latest management system, there was performance accountability in every organization, organization management started using good methods to manage factories, industries and companies also they were using bureaucratic management system in the industry. People saw structure and standard in industrial jobs, workers had more freedom of association with the management, workforce had conferences, higher salary, incentives, health benefits and self-determination. In these last days, the managerial people are reaping the growth and benefit of the previously spawned concept of management professionalism. The notable researchers have created the concept of humanistic, participatory, empowering and managerial enlightenment.

CHAPTER 2
Organizational Change and Managing Adaptation

Change Management represents a large and rapidly growing discipline that is being increasingly deployed on a global scale by corporations, governmental entities, and non-profits. Change Management refers to a structured approach to facilitate the adoption of change by groups and individuals within an organization. Change management is the application of a structured process and tools to enable individuals or groups to transition from a current state to a future state, such that a desired outcome is achieved. When change management is done well, employees feel engaged in the change process and work collectively towards a common objective, and the outcomes are change projects realizing benefits and delivering results. Change management has been defined as the process of continually renewing an organization's direction, structure, and capabilities to serve the ever-changing needs of external and internal customer needs. It is an organizational planned process aimed at involves change stakeholders to accept and embrace changes in their business environment. In some project management contexts, change management refers to a project management process wherein changes to a project are formally introduced and approved.

Change Management differs from Project Management in that Project Management is a technical set of tools and processes applied by a small group of project management professionals. Change Management emphasizes the people-side of change and targets leadership within all levels of an organization including executives, senior leaders, middle managers and line supervisors. Once the decisions are made, the next challenge is implementing the changes throughout the organization. This is, of course, a key responsibility for executives. If the necessary changes are not managed correctly, the result can be a distraught organization filled with a disgruntled staff who exhibit poor performance and only average customer service. All this inevitably leads to greater loss in revenues and lower profit margins. There are more successfully ways to implementing change in an organization.

In the world of computer component systems, direct sale is the primary competitive advantage for selling products or services to prospective traditional and online customers. Whereas, in a computer marketing system, the timely delivery of products is essential to the patrons, the marketing strategy has to be designed and executed with the quick solution to address the problems of patrons in mind. In the following pages, we will discuss the basic characteristics of current management, challenges, and the availability of opportunities. Layout is a pre-requisite of building any strategic structure regardless whether it is a shop, restaurant or office. While sketching layout for different structures, serving different purpose, the designer needs to bear certain things in mind. Those certain things will guide the designer to draw a layout that will serve the purpose of building the structure and will increase efficiency in the work place. Similarly, while making an office layout, there are certain things that need to be focused such as, positioning the workers, their equipment, and the space for transferring information. These things are described below.

While partitioning different departments within an office building, the first thing that needs to be focused is the position of the departments. In a firm, there can be different department and the communication process and communication level within the different departments are not equal. If the departments are located analyzing the communication process and interaction level, it is more likely to increase the productivity of the company and make communication easier and smoother between those departments.

Employees need different sort of equipment while working in the office. For example we can talk about the printer. These equipment need to be placed accordingly. The department which needs to use the machinery the most is more likely to have the machinery in the closest possible position. It will save time for the employee and increase their efficiency level.

In some office the hierarchy structure is still used and if the layout is designed for an office like that, the departments need to locate in a way so that the information can flow flawlessly. Similarly, there are also information that is generated by the CEO to the department head, then to managers and then to the rest of the employees. To make such flow of information smooth and effective, the space should be allocated thoughtfully. Miss-management or failure to arrange the location effectively will result in decreased productivity and slow information passing process.

Industry location problems could seriously affect the overall progress of the business and thus this factor needs to be monitored continuously. Evaluation of the efficiency level of location strategy ensures high level of productivity for the firm. There are typically 4 methods in which the location problems are addressed such as factor-rating method, location break-even analysis, and center of gravity method and transportation model.

Factor rating method is one of the most popular methods for understanding the efficiency of the location strategy. In this method, different key success factor of the location strategy is accumulated and analyzed. This method is typically completed in six steps. In the first step, the key success factors are gathered. Then weight is assigned for each factor. In the next step a scale is developed for each factors, they are scored and then multiplied with the distributed weights. The location with the highest score is announced to be the most effective.

Location break-even analysis is the method that does the cost-volume analysis and they are mostly used in case of industrial location. This method is completed in three steps. First of all, the fixed and variable cost for each location is determined, the cost for each location is plotted and the location for the lowest cost is selected. This method can also be followed to understand the efficiency level of one single form's location.

Center of gravity method mainly finds the distribution center and analyses if the distribution cost is minimized. Some factors are brought into consideration, such as location of the market, volume of goods shipped and also the shipping cost. Transportation model on the other hand analyses the amount need to be shipped from several points of supply to several points of demand. This is supposed to give the firm the minimized total production and shipping cost and also will help to understand if the process they are currently following is effective or not. The purpose of this book is to examine the efficacy of the current security measures of the e-commerce of the Corporate America. To achieve this purpose, the book will use evaluation methodology. The primary objective of an evaluation is to provide useful findings and recommendations to a variety of audiences, including the management of an organization. In addition, the objective of any evaluation is to influence the standard of creating policy by providing empirically driven judgment to assist the management of organization. As such, evaluation is an appropriate methodology for achieving the intended purpose of this book.

In this review, the primary aim is to determine whether the e-commerce company's security procedures ensure proper safeguarding of the assets. To this end, the current book will investigate how current firewall software is protecting the organization's computer operating systems from hackers' malicious attacks. The e-commerce community has defined hackers' infringement into computer operating systems as cybercrime. Cybercrime against e-commerce sites is escalating rapidly, as is the amount of losses. However, the overall dimension of cybercrime remains ambiguous. Thus, security administrators at e-commerce organizations must integrate exceptional security measures to protect both customers and assets.

In this book, risk assessment will be conducted to help verify how the existing firewall is protecting the fixed assets of the e-commerce company. In particular, the book will focus on how the firewall is protecting fixed assets, such as the company's (a) web site, (b) computer hardware, (c) software, (d) networks, (e) servers, (f) propriety information,

(g) email system, and (h) bank accounts. The result of the risk assessment will drive the examination of the company's firewall and current security measures.

A security review commences with risk assessment. A risk assessment is the verification of risks and points of susceptibility. In this book, the primary objective is to conduct a risk assessment of both information assets and knowledge assets to inform the evaluation process. For example, the questionnaires used in this book will determine assets in order to verify potential risks, including (a) information at risk, (b) customers' dossier, (c) proprietary designs, (d) business operations, (e) confidential processes, (f) internal data, (g) prices, (h) executive compensation, and (i) payroll.

The integration of security into computer systems has become inexorable for every e-commerce organizations. All transactions conducted over the Internet involve exchanging packets with other computers. These packets may contain e-mail messages, instant messenger chats, or HTML pages. Moreover, it is common knowledge that packets can contain harmful software or viruses sent from a hacker. For example, hackers can perpetuate a DOS attack to shut down a company's web site. In order to expedite potent security, the practitioner should configure a complex network using a firewall to discourage intruders. Firewalls—either as part of the software or hardware—monitor and filter packets sent to a computer. Firewalls enable e-commerce organizations to rigidly preclude undesired data before their advent into the computer system.

In this book, the purpose is to interpret the findings stemming from a risk assessment and using the results to develop questionnaires that will be used to determine the efficacy of the company's security measures. The questionnaires will be administered to key employees. Employees' office will serve as the physical location for the interviews and fieldwork. Information from interviews will be tabulated and documented in Microsoft Office Excel in order to conduct rigorous testing. Interpreting the responses to the questionnaires will help determine whether the current security measure is effective.

A memorandum will be prepared to document the findings, strengths, and weaknesses. Key employees will then sign the memorandum. The book will also communicate the findings and recommendations to the management, achieving their agreement on the findings and recommendations. A written report will be prepared at the completion of the field work, which will include the applicable findings, commendations, recommendations, estimated cost savings (if identified), and a written management response addressing recommendations. The findings, recommendations, and implementation process will be appended to the body of the evaluation report. The policies and procedures will be prepared to drive the implementation of the recommendations.

E-commerce transactions may lack integrity because hackers may compromise the dossier. When weak security measures are in place, customers may not be aware that third parties have the liberty to read their private information. The company and customers' dossier include information such as credit card numbers, which may be divulged into the wrong hands due to a lack of confidentiality. Another problem is privacy; customers' private information (e.g., bank account numbers) may be unveiled on competitors' or hackers' websites. Lacking potent security, hackers can use software viruses to shut down web sites. The lack of security may permit web site navigators to deny or repudiate their actions while on the Internet. In its annual Internet report, the University of California discovered that approximately eighty-nine percent of participants in one study disclosed that they were somewhat apprehensive about their privacy. Thus, e-commerce companies should be responsible for preventing consumers' information from getting into the hands of cyber criminals.

Hackers have an extensive arsenal of weapons to use when carrying out cybercrimes, including malicious code viruses, worms, Trojan horses, and bad applets that sabotage organizations' operating systems. Hackers also use virus software to sabotage operating systems' integrity. Malicious code viruses change how network systems function and alter documents created on the operating system. The cybercriminal can use hacking and cyber-vandalism to deliberately sabotage, interrupts, vandalizes, or even obliterates a web site.

In addition, online fraudsters often commit credit card fraud or theft—one of the most-feared occurrences and one of the main reasons more consumers do not buy products or services from e-commerce organizations. The most common cause of credit card fraud is a lost or stolen card that is used by online criminal. Criminals can also apply for credit cards using false identities. Organizational employees can steal customers' numbers, or stolen identities can be used to perpetrate credit card fraud on web sites.

Another activity common among online fraudsters is disguising their identities or misrepresenting themselves, which they do by forwarding fake e-mail addresses or pretending to be someone else. Cyber criminals can spoof by redirecting a web link to an address other than the intended one, camouflaging the new site as the intended destination. Similarly, online hackers can produce overall service attacks by using virus software to overwhelm a web site with useless traffic, thereby inundating the network. Such attacks ultimately shut down the e-commerce web site and damage its reputation and customer relationships.

Finally, hackers can use virus software to sniff or monitor e-commerce organizations' information. Sniffing virus software helps hackers capture information traveling over a network, thereby enabling hackers to pilfer proprietary information from anywhere on the network, including e-mail communications, customer dossiers, company files, financial data, and confidential reports. Consequently, secret or personal dossiers are made public. Employees may even perpetrate criminal activities using the organization's sensitive dossiers because they have access or authorization to sensitive dossiers and procedures. Thus, it is clear that e-commerce organizations must effectively deal with a number of potential security issues.

The employees are not required to have on file with an authorized supervisor any privately established identification and passwords to access their computers. The threat is that data about banking relationships may be captured by cyber criminals. Members of the several organizations were found sharing their computer password with each other and this problem still exists today in e-commerce companies. Sixty-six percent of information technology professionals and chief executives confessed that they had allocated their password to coworkers.

The internal control mechanism is so weak, for instance, employees have liberty to take the organization's computer to their individual homes and bring it back to their offices. The cyber-criminal can steal the organization computers and use the data in it to commit fraud. For example, no firewalls or proxy servers were available, and employees are not required to have on file with an authorized supervisor any privately established identification and passwords to access their computers. The e-commerce company also did not include antivirus software in their computer operating systems.

Computer operating systems generally have security strengths because of the built-in username and password requirement that provides a level of authentication. Some operating systems possess access control responsibility that automates user access, denying clients' access to certain areas of the network. For example, operating systems security can control access to selected network paths so that only designated personnel can obtain access to payroll information.

The most common worms and viruses can be avoided by keeping the server and client operating systems and applications up-to-date. Automatic computer security upgrades are offered by Microsoft and Apple. For example, Microsoft continually upgrades Windows server 2003 and windows XP client operating systems to address vulnerabilities discovered by hackers. These improvements are autonomic; when using windows XP on the Internet, users are commonly prompted and informed that operating system improvements are available. Users can simply download these security enhancements free of charge. Application vulnerabilities are also repaired in the same way. For example, users are often invited to visit both the Mozilla browser and Internet Explorer 6.0 web sites for security improvements and patches.

Many organizations depend on application software, including Microsoft Office and all server-side database packages, which contain extensive security management features utilized on networks and intranets to administer access to data files. Academic communities recognize Microsoft software as an operating system as it possesses built-in software firewalls. A software firewall is a packet-monitoring program installed on a computer. People refer to software firewall as a personal firewall. However, several authorities recommend buying and installing additional software firewalls, such as the Norton firewall.

After evaluating the responses to the questionnaires, several weaknesses were identified in the organization under study. For example, no firewalls or proxy servers were available, and employees are not required to have on file with an authorized supervisor any privately established identification and passwords to access their computers. The e-commerce company also did not include antivirus software in their computer operating systems. Furthermore, the vetted responses to the questionnaires indicated that several disturbing occurrences have manifested within the company, including (a) loss of credit card data, (b) loss of data, (c) inadequate system backup, (d) inadequate server backup, (e) loss of electronic monetary funds, (f) loss of payroll data, (g) loss of confidential data, and (h) loss of proprietary information. Thus, the organization's security measures are not performing effectively and need improvement. Computer operating systems and servers are susceptible to attack if not protected with firewalls software, firewall hardware, encryption, and antivirus software. In agreement, The Firewalls and proxy servers are intended to safeguard a company's network as well as the attached servers and clients—just like physical-world firewalls protect operating systems from fires for a limited period.

Based on the findings, several recommendations can be made to enhance security at the company in question. Employees at the e-commerce organization should be required to have on file with an authorized manager privately established identification and passwords to access their computers. Moreover, changes in passwords should require immediate written notification to the authorized management. In addition, the e-commerce company should purchase firewall software, proxy servers, and antivirus software for all computer operating systems. To determine the effectiveness of security, a peer review should be conducted by a team from a similar e-commerce organization; the review should determine whether security measures were suitably designed and are operating effectively.

For example, e-commerce administrator should install Norton AntiVirus in order that e-mail attachments are inspected before any individual clicking on them, and the attachments are discarded if they contain a known virus or worm. After installing the virus software, the employees and security administrator should continue to monitor the computer operating systems. The hackers always create and release viruses on a daily basis; therefore, daily routine updates are needed in order to preclude new threats from being loaded. Automatically, some premium level antivirus software may be set up to update hourly.

Another similar type of virus software, which is more complex and expensive, is an intrusion detection system. Such programs work similarly like anti-virus software in that they identify hacker tools or signature actions. Designed to generate an alarm when such an action is noted, these systems must be monitored by employees or intrusion detection services in order to work appropriately. Sensors set up on a computer network will generate hundreds of alarms, with only a very small percentage being a potential security danger. Regular monitoring and analysis help discard the irrelevant from the potentially harmful. Despite the extra work involved in discarding false alarms, intrusion detection systems also serve as a first line of defense against hacker attacks.

In additional example, a study indicated that seventy-seven percent of the participants in the computer security study indicated their computer operating systems were adequately safeguarded with firewall software and antivirus solution software. Conversely, thirty-three percent commented that their computer operating systems were not adequately safeguarded with firewall and antivirus software. Several organizations may cite wasteful spending was their reason for not protecting the computer operating systems.

To enhance security, the e-commerce company should purchase firewall hardware. Firewalls are software applications that create filters between a company's private network and the Internet. Although firewalls and proxy servers share some similar roles, they are quite dissimilar. The firewall software prevents remote client computers from attacking the internal network of the e-commerce company. Firewall software monitors and validates all incoming and outgoing proprietary information. Every message leaving or entering the network is processed by the firewall software, which verifies if the message meets security standards established by the organization. If the message meets the security requirements, it can be distributed; if it does not, it is blocked. The firewalls software are effective for managing traffic to and from servers and clients, forbidding communications from untrustworthy sources, and permitting other communications from trusted sources to proceed. Firewalls can filter traffic based on packet attributes such as source IP address, destination port, private individual, and type of service. Firewalls can filter viruses that are emanating from the IP address, home personal computers, corporate computers, global computers, domain name of the source, and several other dimensions.

The hardware firewall device is appended to the computer system and functions to filters malicious packets, according to precise monitoring criteria. It has the power to monitor the sender of a packet or the contents of the packet itself (Leon, 2008). Most hardware firewalls are used by organizations to protect local area networks connected to the Internet. The local area networks have default settings that require little or no administrator intervention, and the systems adhere to simple but effective rules that deny arriving packets from a connection that does not originate from an internal request. When an organization requests services from trustworthy organizations, the hardware firewalls will permit connections only from servers at those trustworthy organizations.

A common default setting that people will find on hardware firewalls include DSL and cable modem routers. The DSL and cable modem routers will not communicates with TCP port 445, the most commonly attacked port. The increasing use of firewalls by home, company and government internet users has greatly diminished the effectiveness of virus attacks, and forced hackers to concentrate more on e-mail attachments to dispense worms and viruses. The manufacturer of firewalls designed the software to have established procedures that authenticate traffic, including packet filters and application gateways. With firewalls, unauthorized or dangerous packets to a computer will be annihilated and blocked from entering the computer system. For security purposes, the security administrator may designate packet filters that scrutinize data packets to ascertain whether they are destined for a prohibited port or originate from a prohibited IP address. In order to determine whether the incoming information may be transmitted, the filter is configured to search for the source of information, the port, the packet type, and destination of the information. However, the packet-filtering method is vulnerable to spoofing because authentication is not one of its functions.

An application gateway is another type of firewall software that deliberately filters messages when users request any type of application. The application gateway will not filter messages by source or destination of the communication; rather, it will process a request at the application lever, a remote area from the client computer. In brief, this can compromise operating system performance.

Although hardware firewall costs significantly more than software firewall, either one can effectively safeguard an entire network of computers. Meanwhile, some functions of the software firewall afford the opportunity to filter packets sent to a computer upon access into the computer. The shortcoming is that the software firewall must be separately installed on each computer, which is arduous work that might create problems for a company with multiple computers.

Firewalls operate to decline access by remote client computers to local computers, the primary function of a proxy is to offer controlled access from local computers to remote computers. Several organizations use proxy servers in conjunction with a designated computer to manipulate all messages going into and from the Internet. Security administrators normally use proxy servers to operate as a spokesperson or bodyguard for the organization preferring to use proxy servers to limit access of internal clients to external Internet servers. Proxy servers are commonly referred to as dual home systems because they possess two network interfaces. To internal computers, the proxy server is the same as gateway; to external computers, the proxy server is the same as mail server or numeric address.

Several organizations use proxy servers safeguard a local area network from Internet intruders and preclude internal users from navigating prohibited web servers. The security administrator can make the organization's proxy server available to scrutinize web pages coming from an external Internet server. If the content meets security standards, the web pages will travel to the internal network web server and the client's desktop. By inhibiting users or employees from interacting directly with the Internet, organizations can preclude access to certain categories of sites that are notorious for sending malicious codes, like viruses, bad applets, worms, and Trojan horses. Proxy servers also improve web performance by storing frequently requested web pages locally, reducing upload times, and hiding the internal network's address, thus making it more difficult for hackers or criminal perpetrators to monitor.

The increasing use of firewalls by home, company, and government Internet users has greatly diminished the effectiveness of virus attacks and forced hackers to concentrate more on e-mail attachments to dispense worms and viruses. In regard to security measures, the easiest and least costly way to preclude threats to computer operating systems' integrity is to install anti-virus software. Software programs by McAfee, Symantec, and Norton Antivirus offer inexpensive tools that identify and eliminate the most common types of virus software as they enter a computer as well as annihilate those already available on a hard drive.

Software programs by Trend Micro AntiVirus, McAfee, Symantec and Norton Antivirus offer inexpensive tools to identify and eliminate the most common types of virus software as they enter a computer as well as eradicate the worms already available on a hard drive. The e-commerce administrator should install such a program in order to ensure that e-mail attachments are inspected before any individuals open them; when using such programs, attachments are discarded if they contain a known virus or worm. After installing the virus software, employees and the security administrator should continue to monitor the computer operating systems because hackers create and release new viruses on a daily basis; therefore, daily routine updates should be followed to prevent new threats from being loaded. Some premium-level antivirus software may be set up to update automatically on the hour.

Another more complex and expensive virus software is an intrusion detection system. Such programs work like anti-virus software in that they identify hacker tools or signature actions, generating an alarm when such an action is noted. The employees or intrusion detection services must monitor intrusion detection systems in order to work appropriately. Sensors set up on a computer network will generate hundreds of alarms, with only a very small percentage being a potential security danger. Regular monitoring and analysis help discard the irrelevant from the potentially harmful. Despite the extra work involved in discarding false alarms, intrusion detection systems also serve as a first line of defense against hacker attacks.

In order to diminish security threats, e-commerce firms must create a coherent organization policy that will consider the nature of the risks, the information assets that need safeguarding, and the procedures and technologies required to tackle the risk as well as execution and auditing systems. Policies and procedures are formulated to become the basis for the implementation of the recommendations. The purpose of this procedure is to establish concise guidelines that will provide safe and virus-free computer operating systems for the e-commerce company. This policy will ensure compliance with the organization guidelines on security measures. The goal is to eliminate malicious codes or viruses from the computer operating system.

The e-commerce company has a zero-tolerance for loss of propriety information stemming from an attack by hackers and the potential liability resulting from such occurrences. Management has the inherent responsibility to provide appropriate resources to maintain a virus-safe web site environment. The management must enforce the implementation of the recommendations previously discussed. In other words, management should purchase firewall software, proxy servers, firewall hardware, and antivirus software and load them on all computer operating systems. In addition, employees should be required to have on file with an authorized manager privately established identification and passwords to access their computers. Moreover, changes in passwords must require immediate written notification to the authorized management. Employees must maintain awareness of the requirement for security safe web site, servers, and computer operating systems.

The Virus Software Prevention Plan (VSPP) ensures that a written plan will be developed and implemented outlining responsibilities for all levels of management. The VSPP will consist of seven components as prescribed by the management. These components include management implementation of the recommendations, analysis, monitoring, recordkeeping, audit, attack investigation, review and reporting. Designated security administrator, who has been assigned security safety functions, will have oversight responsibilities for VSPP.

In order to create the initiatives of the VSPP, certain positions shall be vested with certain responsibilities. Security safety committee, executive management, security safety staff, supervisors, and employees are listed as points of reference. The security administrator will be responsible for: (a) Implementing security recommendation, operations and practices as developed by security safety staff. (b) Consistently applying and enforcing security safety and computer rules, methods, procedures, policies, and standards—providing, replacing, and maintaining servers and computer operating systems as necessary. (c) Reinforcing security safety behavior in accordance with the approved plan; and (d) periodically retraining employees in the act of security safety, firewalls maintenance, procedures, and policies to maintain general awareness.

In addition, the security administrator will be accountable for: (a) promptly reviewing facts and circumstances surrounding virus attacks, including the mandated telephone reporting and documentation. (b) Conducting and documenting virus attack investigations. (c) Attending security safety and malicious code training and education classes as defined by the organization's plan; and (d) including but not limited to malicious code attack and investigation as well as supervisors' responsibility for firewall improvement.

This scholar has discussed how transactions on the e-commerce may lack integrity because the online hackers can compromise users' dossiers. When weak security is in place, customers may not be aware that the third parties have liberty to access their private information. The companies and customers' dossiers may be subject to lack of confidentiality. Another problem is privacy; customers' private information may be available on competitors' web sites. The e-commerce company should prevent the consumers' information from getting into the hands of cyber criminals. Without effective security, web sites may be shut down because of the invasion of software virus. The lack of security may permit web site navigators to deny or repudiate their actions while on the internet.

The year was in the 1984 when a 19-year-old young man by the name of Michael Dell successfully inaugurated the Dell Computer Corporation. The business management scope was based on the concept of selling directly to the prospective patrons. Consequently, Dell enjoys the privileges of having no retailers or intermediaries in its business transactions. As a result, the customers enjoyed the avoidance of markups because the distributors and retailers were out of the loop. In time, Lee Walker, a 51-year-old venture capitalist and now a former CEO of Dell Computer Corporation, became the ardent mentor of Michael Dell. Known for his fatherly persona at the company, he was able to memorize all of the employees' names. As fate would have it, Michael Dell accumulated all of the managerial, entrepreneurial and executive acumen he now has from Mr. Walker. Thanks to Mr. Walker's transfer of knowledge and assistance, Michael Dell is now a paragon of a charismatic executive. As a result, he is a strong believer in motivating and obtaining the honor and loyalty of the workforce. Dell Computer Corporation hired several hall of fame boards of directors when the company was incorporated in 1988.

A good leader exemplifies someone who will bring peace, bond of unity and harmony, thereby destroying any hostile dividing wall between the corporate members. In like manner, in the Dell Computer Corporation, according to the belief of its top management, it is better to distribute authority and power among the corporate members because this will lead to organizational success. Furthermore, Dell is persuaded that the main focus and mindset of the top management should be that one of accomplishing corporate goals because this is tantamount to triumph for internal and external stakeholders. There should be availability of regards, honor and decorum among the top management. Moreover, there should be constant interaction of one accord on the goals and objectives of the company. Consequently, customers state that they are treated with utmost regard and the following are the steps that lead to such acclaim: any computer problem originating from the customer goes to design engineers then to factory where the problem is resolved with immediate effect. It is the belief of the management that timeliness in response to the patrons' issues makes Dell highly competitive against its competitors.

Dell management is known to interact intensively with its workforce, to the fact that all employees are made aware of the state of the economy, whether it is positive or negative, the outstanding company modes of operations, company forthcoming agendas, and how to accomplish corporate goals. The faster medium of accumulating and utilization of informational content, computer component and software now allow managers to make adequate decision making. The computer information process is now available for management hence they can use it to improve organizational, technical and administering competitiveness.

Michael Dell conducted town hall meetings at various locations annually and spent a lot of time answering questions. Company successes were celebrated at get-togethers and via e-mail communications, congratulating teams on big account triumphs or other special achievements. Best practices in one area were shared with other areas. Much communication took place in real time via extensive e-mail and the company intranet". Involving the workforce is a good idea, however, it needs to be done for the right reasons and it is necessary for management to take responsibility for conducting the process. Meetings and focus groups comprising of employees and management are held to encourage opinions and recommendations to be offered, dialogue, and constructive criticism. When management considers recommendations and bonds of trust are created that allows employees to feel gratitude and valued and in turn gives the employees irreplaceable recognition.

Michael Dell had visualized, the direct-to-the-customer strategy that gave the company a significant cost and profit margin advantage over competitors that manufactured various PC models in volume and reserved their distributors and retailers stocked with ample inventories. However, it was necessary for Dell Computer to purchase existing storage businesses to be operated as subsidiaries. Further, autonomous management teams should direct the employees and the management team must develop the modern vision and energy. In 2000 there was major problem with several computer companies that resulted in lost market opportunities but on the other hand Dell Computer Corporation had massive increases in net income that accrued to $35 billion in the fiscal year 2003. One thing to note is that Dell Corporation was successful because the organization has adopted the system of continuous strategies and reapplies the ingredient of the strategy for years.

The model that entices and motivates the workforce to fulfill the broad-spectrum of company goals and objectives has balanced the management concept of Dell. One thing is abundantly clear; purposeful compliance of employees with workplace policies and procedures and assigned tasks is necessary, hence the workforce must routinely and enthusiastically work at it. Most importantly, employees should not pretend to work only when they know they are being watched. Conversely, the focal point of Dell management is its sensitivity to the combination of customer and supplier. Hence, the company's business model was revamped; new manufacturing capacity, infrastructure, and more management staff were added and costs were drastically cut. It is important to note that the founder anticipated Dell Computer to become the greatest PC Company on a global scale. The commerce on the Internet possesses some reward as opposed to traditional store retailing. However, online patrons might pay exorbitant prices without thinking about the quality. The way customers who shop online think about the quality of online products differs, however, they indicate their likeness and contentment by their ability to communicate on the web site, the timeliness of products arrival and strong preparation of the company to deal with a potential dilemma.

The Dell Computer Company adopted e-commerce to stimulate customer service, enjoyment and satisfaction.

Additionally, the company developed twenty-four hour Internet customer service and technical support. Patrons are treated with utmost respect via amicable communications conducted through the online, telephone and email channels. Punctuality and alacrity is the essence of the business, thus patrons are competitively treated with positive courtesy. This is done by constantly making on-time deliveries. Dell knows in detail, the logistics of efficient product transportation to the individual customer from coast to coast. Conversely, Dell does not operate through a warehouse; no inventory and orders from the customers are immediately assembled upon requisition.

Consumers usually start the transaction of purchasing a computer component via the phone or through the Internet on www.dell.com. It normally takes three days for the employees of Dell Computer to do credit checks, and view patrons' customized orders, but generally it takes no more than five days to ship orders to the patrons. One thing about shopping online is that the online organization offers similar products to the consumers that they would otherwise not have thought about with the absence of the databases that collect customers' information, such as favorites and prior transactions. Conversely, another side effect that may affect customers is that technical problems, glitches, web-site problems or server disconnections may impinge on the ability to complete transactions. Nevertheless, the advantages of online shopping though include the ability to conduct transactions for 24 hours a day, seven days a week, which is particularly good for several patrons who are preoccupied with other daily activities.

Furthermore, Dell Company operates on just-in-time acquisition of computer parts. Because of this no-warehouse innovation, Dell is a cost effective competitive computer corporation. Accountability for the computer quality assurance is classic at Dell Computer Corporation because an individual employee is responsible for assembly of a complete set of computer hardware hence culpability for computer glitch could be traced to that individual. Conversely, Dell Computer Company does not use retailers because it is less cost efficient to do so, and Dell strives to remain a low cost organization, therefore time and funds are not wasted. A casual onlooker would believe that Dell Computer Corporation operates an effective business.

Dell's system of business depends on build-to-order production, partnerships with suppliers, just-in-time inventories, and direct sales to patrons, good customer service, technical support, Internet savvy and e-commerce technology. As a matter of fact, Dell Computer Company became triumphant in business because of their revolutionary system that goes against the norm of business operations. It hires employees who are mindful of asking intelligent questions, inquisitive, teachable, and adventurous. Applicants are severely scrutinized because Dell tries to maintain and retain goal oriented, industrious, resourceful, inventive and imaginative individuals. In addition, Dell wants employees that can cope with organizational changes.

If an employee wants tenure, employment longevity, the ability to contribute ideas or technical breakthrough, and room for advancement, Dell may be the right place, but if complacency or the status quo is preferred by the applicant, Dell is definitely not the right place. However, Dell permits all employees to implement their franchise to critique the way operations are being discharged and therefore, employees may offer innovative ways or ideas on how to better discharge operations. Thus, Dell honors the culture of progression and improvement. The management of Dell Computer Corporation has amassed great industrial growth. This is predicated upon the resourcefulness and solidarity among the employees; the workforce is also very satisfied, motivated and confident. Moreover, Walker had a lot of impact on the employees as he treated them like part of his own family. In addition, ensuring that employees were retained and motivated, Michael Dell a transformed charismatic executive went ahead and motivates his workforce. Therefore, employees gave their loyalty and respect. At Dell, there is a team-oriented environment where people discharge their daily duties in teams of two employees; they also receive, assemble and put the products in the boxes heading to patrons' locations. Teams were assigned productivity goals and objectives that had to be achieved. Thus, Dell installed signboards to depict hourly performance scores for opponent teams' members to monitor and compete with each other in order to meet productivity goals. Accordingly, the manager at Dell is responsible for conducting yearly employee performance evaluations.

Dell allocates profit sharing incentives to stimulate team members' productivity. As part of incentive programs, the members of its workforce are also stockholders. They have stock option grants and a 401k plan and a matching program that pays employees in stock. Employees are also entitled to the company's health insurance. Employee compensation and incentives are now fixed corresponding to growth and value of Dell's business and are scrutinized by the organization's return on invested capital (ROIC). There are several ways to reward employees hence companies do not need to spend a lot of money rewarding employees.

There are ways to continually keep employees motivated that just require a little of a managers time to complete. The following are some suggestions for managers: (1) praise employees on the spot for a job well done (2) have an open door policy day where your desk is clear and employees come in to speak with you (3) establish a clear career path for employees within the organization so they feel like there is opportunity for growth (4) celebrate achievements for an employee or groups of employees (5) thank individuals in front of other employees during group meetings for a job well done or particular contributions.

The open door policy should be emphasized as one of the better ways of employee motivation. It is very important for managers to always know the personal goals, dreams and current happenings of their employees. Thus, Hawthorne studies made it clear that when management is proficient on the concept of human relations he/she would acclaim better treatment of employees; mentor oriented, and care giving. In addition, management who trust his/her subordinate would extend interpersonal skill to the workforce this management would also apply benefits and financial incentives to normalize employees' performance.

Dell Computer Company is one of the major companies that demonstrated the superb initiative in incorporating the Internet and e-commerce technology into daily business transactions. In 1999, Michael Dell commented to 1,200 patrons the world will be transformed forever by the Internet. The Internet will be your enterprise. If your enterprise is not enabled by allocating customers and suppliers with abundant information, your enterprise will go into bankruptcy. People might ask this question: what are the opportunities and advantages that Dell derives from Internet? The followings are the major benefits and good fortune: (1) open up servers business (2) lower cost of transaction, (2) lower cost of conversation between customer and companies, (4) business to business (B2B) commerce, (5) competitive advantages eradication (6) increase market share (7) create impressive performance at reduced price (8) Dell's competitors curtail their server prices (9) Dell's competitors' margins were sabotaged and they could not fund other product lines.

Dell enjoys so many advantages because its management seized the opportunity of association with outstanding suppliers, which led to its use of just-in-time inventory. This allowed Dell to procure substantial cost advantages and its products were quickly place in the marketplace. Dell also created the opportunity for its patrons and employees to be able to converse about individual experiences and exchange ideas on the Internet. Meanwhile, the data drilling from these conversations enabled Dell to foretell the demand on different computer types. It is interesting to note that management caught the idea that customers favored storage devices from online discussions among corporate customers. Therefore, organization management believed that it was Dell's job to sort out all the brand new technology integrating into the marketplace and help navigate customers to alternatives and solutions most pertinent to their needs.

Dell is a company that sells product directly to the consumers therefore they know what customers prefer; they know the immediate feedback that pertains to the quality or design anomalies. Similarly, the organizational management should possess the capability to describe, prophesy, handle, and solve dilemmas. To combat any iota of challenges from its global customers, it became a customary agenda for Dell to use inspector personnel to do the task of crosschecking and auditing one of the most important aspects of its business, the quality control of the finished products. Here, it should be noted that Dell Computer Company is a certified member of the in famous ISO 9002 quality standard. The management at Dell anticipates the challenges that might materialize, which is the reason why the engineers of Dell's suppliers pays visitation at Dell's plant whenever new products are needed to be assembled. In essence, engineer's job is to listen to customer's issues, concerns, praises and makes adjustments. In the event of a recall or a similar disastrous incident the engineer and certain Dell employees have the advantage of stopping the assembly process and correcting the dilemma.

One knows that some customers have developed a habit of complaining, on the other hand, they don't need to give in to the temptation to murmur and complain and they need to set a guard over their mouth. Consequently, several computer companies face a series of complaints, service calls, higher technical-support costs, and patron down times. Dell handled these challenges through the creation of Dell Talk (DT), an online forum where (IT) professionals and computer users interact on computer problems and other criteria. It is interesting to note that there is presently an availability of hundreds of thousands of registered users that correspond with each other on DT. Dell Company uses the information from the DT to prevent or correct computer problems.

The challenges of the PC problems faced by Dell Computer Corporation were considered as an opportunity to improve product quality and reliability. By and large the suppliers were made aware of the faulty component redesign or instructed to correct future recurrences of the problem. For instance, Compaq Computer Company was leveraging with their substantial margin on servers sales to finance desktops, this company also embarked on notebook price reduction; in essence, these challenges were coming against Dell Company from Compaq Computer. However, Dell Company won the victory over the challenges and price war from Compaq Computer. Dell was victorious in this battle because it had a PC account with corporate patrons whereby the competitor did try but failed to wrestle the account away from Dell's ownership. Furthermore, Dell Company was confronted with the challenge of entering the market of servers. Consequently, because of Dell Company business prowess it surmounted the obstacle and was able to enter the server business, which gave them the competitive edge. Consequently, it is the responsibility of Company management to use game theory strategies and principles as deterrent against competitive attack from rival company. Let us now peruse the management theory and practice within the modern era.

Mayo extended the principles of performance and motivation. He mentioned that the components of performance and motivation are harmony, cohesion, team spirit, and camaraderie. Mayo encouraged company to consider using a hierarchy chart and policies as a framework that would allow workers to be motivated to produce satisfactorily. In terms of Dell's business management, the concept of Mayo and others are abundantly apparent and incorporated. Furthermore, Mooney and Reiley advocated for correction of human difference, unhappiness, poverty and dissatisfaction (Wren, 2005). Apparently, the management theory and practice models within the modern era are basically the total quality management (TQM). Thus, Demming and Pareto advocated that the responsibility of an organization's quality control rests on the shoulders of the upper management and they should be held responsible for the elimination of quality defects. Furthermore, Demming and Pareto said that in every organization, management should scrutinize the segment that is notorious for quality defects, develop a finding, create recommendation and execute the remedy. Having said that, let us look into the organizational behavior and theory.

The doctrine of human relations movement basically advocated for management to assume the role of caretaker of employees, not production. Instead of organization hierarchy management must focus on employee betterment, motivation and financial incentives. The human relation movement was supportive of organizational behavior that included social skills, human skills, acclimating employees to the new environment, encouraging union membership in order to minimize employee powerlessness, and participative executive. Thus, business enterprises are looking for capable forward-looking managers who could apply the combination of management thought from the past with new strategies so that their company could be competitive in the global economy. In essence organizational behavior comprises collaborative, open, communicative, cohesive, supportive, objective and adaptive aspects. The next paragraph will show us the role of science in systems management.

The psychology discipline would provide managers with better interpersonal skills and the knowledge of human relations because this is the panacea that helps one to comprehend and respect each member of the workforce. At the same token, the sociology discipline would help managers to be proficient in motivating employees. One should be reminded that an organization has to achieve goals and objectives and management must know how to motivate its employees in order to do so. Moreover, social psychology tells us how employees are affected by changes that occur in organization environment. Similarly, company policies could be drafted to stipulate improvement through training, awareness seminars or mentor programs. Anthropology is a social science that preaches about diversities, social customs, people's beliefs and people's values, which we can find in our today's organization. Consequently, managers must understand and value the diverse cultural ethics. These philosophies have endured the test of time and are the foundation of all organizations. Managers of company have an important fiduciary responsibility to the organization's stakeholders; therefore they must be conscientious in managing the organizational resources. Economic truism is that the research on the management thought must proceed with continuous improvement including researching for the best managerial fiduciary duties.

Prudent business management practice suggests that Dell Computer Corporation should continue to focus on its inventiveness of using e-commerce to amplify supply chain management in order get increased demand, productivity and assembly efficiencies. We recommend the continuation of one thing that the consumers like about Dell Computer, which is the frequent rapport with all patrons through the telephone, and the web sites. Meanwhile, frequent communication will lead to repeat purchases, encourage word of mouth advertisements by the customers, lower advertisement costs and increase Dell's net income.

A standing example of what Dell does better than other organizations is its awareness of consumers demand in terms of the computer components that people always purchase or dislike. Dell started e-commerce sales in 1995 with immediate effect and automatic alacrity, the revenue from the sales reached one million dollars per day, three million dollars per day by 1997, fourteen million dollars per day by 1998 and sky rocketed to thirty five million dollars per day by 1999. Dell Computer Corporation was successful mainly because "the company's strategy was constructed around a number of core components: build-to-order manufacturing, partnerships with suppliers, just-in-time inventories, direct sales to customers, accolade-winning customer service and technical support, and pioneering use of the Internet and e-commerce technology. Dell is on the right path in its business management but the organization could do better by installing kiosks at every departmental store on a global scale.

We have seen the systems of management, the natures of challenges, and the opportunities at Dell Computer Corporation. One is now familiar to the pragmatic model of staying above competition in the business world of computer component systems. We have seen how direct sale, just-in-time production, and zero inventory stockpile enhances Dell competitive advantage for selling products to the prospective customers. Another thing that is abundantly clear in a computer marketing system is the propensity for customers to like quality and timeliness in delivery of product.

CHAPTER 3
Engage Management Team in Strategic Planning and
Development

The book points out the continual need for
management to watch for better ways to blend the
economic inputs of land, labor and capital to better
meet the needs of external and internal stakeholders.
This is especially important as we become more of a
global economy. Historically and presently the
successful blending of economic resources is a
necessary part of management. Whether there are
incremental changes in a particular industry or a
major leap in technology the astute manager needs to
consider using them. Communication is always
important, but it is critical in a changing business
environment. One has to make every effort to ensure
that all employees understand the hard choices that
have been made. Talk to them about your competitive
strategy and the changes you want to make. Make
them a part of it so that they can assume a degree of
ownership in the situation. Ask for their ideas and
input.

Communicate your goals and direction to every
level of the company. Use sincere language, such as: I
fully comprehend that things are going to be different
from what they have been in the past, but I'm
committed to ensuring that we make it through these
tough times, and I'm counting on you to help me
make it happen. Here's what I need from you. Then
tell them. Building upon the initial ways in which you
share information with your employees during normal
and abnormal circumstances one has to consider
developing a concurrent communication strategy to
remind people about the nature of the organizational
changes that are occurring, the expectations, and the
progress that is being made. In today's uncertain

business environment, employees quickly lose their motivation if they are not involved and kept informed of changes going on around them. The less they are informed, the more their performance is negatively impacted. They may believe that there are hidden significant changes, especially when it comes to their job security. With open communication, honesty is built and the most important link between you and your people trust.

Communicate what decisions are and, as uncomfortable as it may be, communicate what you do not know by promising that they will get to know as soon a s one the information is available. They will respect you for your honesty. Failing to address the difficult questions, questions people may already be asking each other and their peers, does not make the issues go away. Encourage every employee to talk to you about any concerns they may have. Establish a culture of open communication, where people feel free to speak up without fear of losing their jobs. Consistently ask for ideas and suggestions from employees. Encourage them to speak openly about every single thing that might hold your organization back. Ask them to come forward to identify any service flaws that might exist, any wasteful spending they see, ways to streamline operations and any other areas where you need help.

While one may not genuinely have the time to move slowly, changing a situation too quickly will create chaos for your organization. You may feel your people are ready to respond to change, but they may not be able to absorb the changes as quickly as you like. It takes time to assimilate new information, learn new systems or procedures, and to do things in a new and different way. Give your staff time to understand the first wave of changes before introducing more. There are some managers who prefer a single big macro change rather than several small ones. They feel if everyone learns the game plan all at once, they can get on with the business at hand. They believe that disruption continues during the change process whether the changes are big or small.

Unfortunately, the reality is that most people are shocked by any major change. The bigger the change, the bigger the shock! If there needs to be a major change, try to anticipate the reaction and prepare your staff to the best of your ability. This empathetic approach will help everyone concerned in the long run. You know your people, so think about what would be best for them. Keep in mind that while you may be committed to the changes, others will not have had the time to recognize the problem and understand the need for the changes. You will be setting yourself up for misunderstanding. You must make sure they understand what your needs and expectations are. Try to introduce changes incrementally, if possible. Remember, it's important to move at a pace that will ensure you meet your business goals while giving your people the opportunity to process the changes for themselves. Recognize that change affects each individual differently. Some people are more adaptable than others. Many top performers will roll up their sleeves to make things work, moving out of their comfort zone instantly. Others may be completely overwhelmed. Let them know you understand the challenges they are facing and that you are there to help them through it. Here, remember the importance of open communication. Keep your door open to allow people to come in to discuss any apprehension. Provide a comfortable environment where people can air their concerns.

Human beings are basically creatures of habit. They like doing things the same way. Doing things differently takes them out of their comfort zones. Some people may resist and hold back their team and, consequently, your company. Talk to any person who comes to work with a chip on his or her shoulder. Ask the person who is making negative remarks and pulling down morale to refrain from doing so. Explain that everyone is working hard pull together and deliver their best performance each day. Ask them what you can do to help them. It is up to you as their leader to maintain employee morale through change. Set the tone; be a role model and be an example for others to follow. During tough times people will always watch how their leader is acting. Don't let your guard down when it comes to your attitude. When the economy is down, you have to be up. To reduce the loss of productivity during change, make sure your people have the necessary skills to succeed. Training must be a top priority. The time and money you invest in training will eventually pay off in increased profits and service quality. As you look at the changes you plan to implement, ask yourself these training-related questions: What is the level of competence needed to support the changes in our company and help us make it through these challenging times? What training will be needed to bring the staff up to that level of competence? What training is needed on new products, procedures, and especially product support? It is the area where you are likely to make the most profit in the environment.

Don't treat training as though it is the flu, if your staff hangs around together long enough, they will catch it. Training is the vaccine that helps to eliminate the stress common during change. It demonstrates that you appreciate their efforts, want them to feel as though they are a strong part of your team, and also that you plan on keeping them working for you. In essence, training gives your employees a shot in the arm. Meeting the demands placed upon people during the change process requires managing job pressure for yourself and others. What is occurring in the construction industry is serious, but the stress can be reduced by keeping an effort to maintain high morale. For example, one dealer holds an annual customer event. Employees and their families are included as well as customers' families. In spite of the tough economy, this smart dealer recognizes the importance of continuing this management/employee and customer relationship building activity. Another way to alleviate job pressure is to find simple ways to celebrate even the smallest successes. They will pay off big.

Making those hard choices, meeting the challenges head on, and adapting to change with new ways of doing business is the only way to go. No one wants to be extinct.

Unfortunately, we sometimes (even unknowingly) put up our own roadblocks to success. If there is one word that captures the essence of what is occurring in the world today, its change. Downsizing, reorganizing, and cutting costs, are now the norm for survival. No industry is exempt; there are no sacred cows. Even the most venerable and conservative institutions are undergoing significant change just to survive. For this industry, in spite of the improvement that many equipment distributors are reporting, a full recovery is not predicted to occur in the immediate future. For those who have made a conscious decision to make it through these tough times, their survival instincts have kicked in. They have decided to meet these challenges *head on* and *move* forward. They have assessed what changes they can control and which ones they cannot. By adopting this mind-set, they are in a better position to meet additional challenges they will confront as they strive to carry their dealer organization forward. Today's distributor will have to get even tougher to make the hard choices and difficult decisions that will continue to face them in the months ahead. They will have to dig in their heels and fight. Accepting that the world has changed and knowing that the organization must change as well is the first step in a long process. What worked in the past will not necessarily work in the new business environment. Smarter decisions will have to be made, new ways of doing business will have to be uncovered, and the required organizational changes will have to be made to ensure survival and what constitutes the new success.

The entire management team needs to be involved with creating your competitive strategy and on board with the changes needed to implement. Introduce change gradually whenever possible. Share the role expected of them and provide a detailed set of actions. Ensure they understand that they are the coaches who will spur the team forward, and their job is to make sure your entire team is aligned with your competitive strategy. Remind them to think and act as dynamic leaders who will provide the inspiration and encouragement to your entire workforce. Follow the example of a major construction equipment manufacturer who has established a change centre in its headquarters. Appoint top performers to be on your change team to lead the way to deploy the change management process. Let them know you understand that they already have a heavy workload, but you are confident they can help make a difference in your company. Choose people who have high levels of credibility in the company; give them direct access to customers. Let the team know it is expected to help identify problems and focus on offering solutions. Use the motto: For every problem there is a solution, not only with your team, but throughout the company. As problems occur during the onset of change implementation, ask the team to help. New ways of doing things rarely occur without glitches, so ask them to brainstorm ways to identify and solve problems even before they present themselves. Change Masters are people who know how to conceive and lead productive and effective projects, initiatives or ventures that bring new ideas into use. Change takes numerous and diverse form: product innovation, new business enterprise, social change or social venture, organization culture shift, implementation of new technology or work arrangements organizational restructuring or improvement effort. Or move to a new business model. Yet regardless of the type of change, there are a generic set of skills found in the people who lead successful change efforts. To stay ahead of this changing environment, firms need to stimulate more innovation, enterprise, and initiative. They must place more emphasis and value on individuals, who - in the right circumstances - come up with innovations. Firms must invest in people and long-term profitability related to taking a lead in innovation.

Integrated organizations are highly innovative and change oriented; they are willing to move beyond received wisdom, combine ideas from diverse sources, and embrace change as an opportunity. Firms invest in people; individuals may initiate ideas, but teams carry them forward. Firms incentivize initiative, and success comes not from domination but flexibility. High-innovation companies are also exemplary in human-resource practices. Problems are seen as wholes, related to larger wholes, and challenges to established practices. Segmented organizations are innovating-smothering and anti-change. They compartmentalize actions, events, and problems, and keep pieces and persons isolated; innovation is inhibited at every step of the solution-search process. Problems are seen as narrowly as possible and independent of context and connections to other problems. Past structures and procedures dominate the future. The organizations are likely to be large, segmented, and hierarchical. Nevertheless, four change patterns in less-innovating companies are identified. In such firms, there is a tension between desire for innovation and blocking it.

Three skills are needed to manage innovation in integrated environments: power skills; ability to manage problems associated with use of teams and employee participation; and understanding how change is designed and constructed. Needed power tools are supplies information, resources, and support. Supporting the circulation of power are open communication systems, network-forming arrangements, and decentralization of resources. Successful and flourishing corporations will master the art of change: creating a new climate encouraging new procedures and possibilities, anticipating and responding to external pressures, and being responsive to new ideas from inside the organization. The challenge for innovative companies is energizing the grass roots, or to combining the necessity of routine jobs with the possibility of employees contributing to innovation. Needed for innovation is the development of a (parallel participative organization) within the formal hierarchy of a company.

Technology innovation, Organizational structures, Competitive advantages, Employee development, Corporate entrepreneurship, Human resource management, Teamwork, Flexible structures, Resource management, Organizational communication, Change strategies, Management theory, Organizational change, Firm integration, Innovation process. Innovations begins with someone being aware enough to sense a new need which comes from focusing time and attention t things going on in

the environment . Change Masters adept at anticipating the
need for change as well as leading it. They sense new ideas or
appetites emerging on the horizon. They also sense weakness
and problems before they represent full-blown threats. They
see the opportunities when external forces change – new
technology capabilities, industry upheavals and regulatory
shifts. Change Masters are likely to emerge in companies
already open to change. They are pace-setters; in contrast,
they resist anything new or different. It is self-reinforcing
cycle; those already successful at change create the
circumstances that make it easier for people to sense the
need for the next changes, because they have opened minds
and broken through walls. When people are encouraged to
tune in all the time, to be conscious of the context, and to
become restlessly dissatisfied, they are likely to be jarred by
change. Mindless habitual behavior is the enemy of
innovation. Change Masters begin by being mindful. It is one
thing to sense opportunity on the horizon; an additional
mental act of imagination is needed to find a creative ne
response to it. Change Masters take all inputs about needs
and opportunities and use it to shake up reality a little, to get
an exciting new idea of what is possible to break through the
old pattern and invent a new one. Creativity is a lot like
looking at the world through a kaleidoscope. You look at a
set of elements the same ones everyone else sees but the
reassemble those floating bits and pieces into an enticing
new possibility. Innovators shake up their thinking as though
their brain is a kaleidoscope. Innovators reframe the
situation; reset the kaleidoscope on a new pattern which
then becomes the new convention of everyone else. A raw
idea that emerges from kaleidoscope must be shaped into
theme that makes the idea comes out. Ideas do no Lunch
productive changes until they become a theme around which
others begin to improvise, a vision that raises aspiration.
Leaders must wake people out of inertia. They must get
people excited about some things they have never seen
before, something that does not exist. The theme provides a
setting for a story that has to come to life, to raise aspiration
and inspire action. A vision is not just a picture of what

could be, it is an appeal to our better selves and a call to become something more. It reminds us that the future does not descend likes stage set; future is constructed from history, desires and decisions.

As every entrepreneur knows a great idea is not enough. Potential Change Masters must sell the idea more widely; attract the right backers and supporters, entice investors and defenders, and get buy-in from stakeholders in a position to help or harm the venture at later stages. The newer the idea, the more critical this coalition building becomes. Most of them concerns reluctance or outright resistance to change form the key stakeholders and not just the external ones. Coalition building requires an understanding of politics of change and the skills of community organizers. Instead of trying to recruit everyone at once, change masters seek the minimum number of investors necessary to launch the new venture and the champion it when they need help later. Coalitions are fragile, especially when they contain people who look to see which way the political wind is blowing. Top management might withdraw their support if organizational opposition swells instead of declining. Thus, change masters try to widen their coalition – to move people up a continuum toward more active support, if they were neutral, and to the neutral zone if they were opponents.

Once the coalition backers is in place, change masters enlist others in turning the dream into reality. Too often executive announce a plan, launch a task force, and then simply hope that people find answers; instead of offering a dream, stretching their horizons and encouraging people to do the same. In contrast, the areas where people feel that there are in charge of creating future always seem to hum with communication. People cluster to help each other over rough spots. There is a team identity and maybe even a team name. The team has deadlines that are considered milestones whose accomplishment can be celebrated. Leaders now shift their role in the drama of change to the lead actor to produce-director. They bring on stage the rest of the improvisational actors who take task of translating an idea into implementation, a promise into prototype. There are two parts of this job: team-building and team-nurturing. The first consists encouraging the actors to feel like a team with ownership of the goals and a team identity that motivates performance- like sports team that wants to win. The second involves care and feeding of the team as it does it works – to support the team, provide coaching and resources and patrol the boundaries within which the team can freely operate. Successful teamwork is determined not just by the personalities of the people on the team or the particular process they use, but by whether or not the team is linked appropriately to the resources they need from the wider world around them.

One of the mistakes leaders make in change process is launch them and leave them. There are many ways new venture or change initiatives get derailed. This tempts those involved in change process to give up, forget it, and chase the next enticing rainbow. Stop the initiatives so soon and by definition; this is failure. Stay with it through initial hurdles; make appropriate adjustments and mid-course corrections and this will lead to success. Of course if the process takes too long and one has to return to the beginning and monitor the environment again, recheck assumptions look at the way theme is being played out and reset the vision. Constant monitoring is important to keep ideas on track or to redirect them if circumstances change and they often do. There are four common problems that may arise in the middle of developing new products, implementing new process or getting new ventures off the ground: forecasts fall shorts, unexpected obstacles pop up, momentum slows and critics get louder. Critics and skeptics can be internal or external. Leading change can be compared to pushing a boulder up a hill; it takes muscle-power and determination to never let go, or the boulders will roll down and will crush everything.

Remembering to recognize, reward and celebrate accomplishment is the final critical leadership skill. Organizations that desire initiative and innovation thrive on celebration. Creative organizations with their spirit of fun are likely to celebrate everything in sight including just the fact that it is Friday afternoon. Some are better that other at publicizing accomplishment that give change leaders and their team members that warm glow that comes from being recognized by other members of their team members of their community. Recognition is important not only for its motivational pat on the back possible who has done it and what talents reside in the community gene pool. Once the project is complete, make sure to take time to celebrate the accomplishment with team members who made it happen. Organizational change is a perpetual process, so after celebration begin tuning into the environment again to see what next steps are needed and begin right away.

The seven skills of change masters correspond roughly to the phase of the change projects. The first two involves generating ideas, the next two selling ideas and the final three developing and implementing ideas. But this is not to suggest that there is an orderly sequence one carefully steps at a time. In fast moving industries, where innovation is improvisational theatre opportunities become them before the need to document; the producer starts the play while still finding the backers and the team celebrate milestones while ending is still undetermined. Sometimes set of people share responsibilities and sometimes people enter after the idea has already been formulated sometimes they hand it off to another leader to pick up. Skilful leaders in receptive environment can speed up the pace of change, but they cannot altogether avoid the hard work of convincing other to join them in mastering change.

In cognizance of the fact that for several decade people lived and conducted their daily activities without universal necessities and luxuries such as vehicles, electricity, televisions, radios, and telephones, people still survived the ordeal. Conversely, the situation may be deplorable for many of us in this modern age, for instance, in a catastrophe, where these necessities were suddenly taken out of our possession. During the pre-industrial epoch when modern science and technology was non-existent; people did not have electricity in their houses, and subsequently had no laundry appliances.

There were very few commuters with the absence of motor vehicles and travel to places of interest was extremely limited unless it was a migration. There was no radio to listen to or television to watch which led to people having to seek other creative ways of entertaining themselves. Communication channels were also very restricted because of the nonexistence of telephones, computers, Internet and wireless technology. Many of us would not be able to survive under such monotonous and relatively harsh conditions. Consequently, because many of us use our motor vehicles for commuting, electricity for household and everyday use, and advanced communication mediums for exchange of ideas, it should be recognized by society that with the advent of the industrial revolution and scientific and technological advancements, life was made a great deal more effortless, efficient and enjoyable. The remainder of this passage will consider the effects of the industrial revolution on the textiles industry.

The industrial revolution came into existence approximately between 1750 and 1850. It has resourcefully altered the mode of business operations in many organizations and has spawned new management thought processes that have radically transformed and modernized management systems. Furthermore, with the industrial revolution came the advent of scientific and technological advances, which benefited society tremendously and transformed almost every aspect of human culture, not only the physical characteristics, but also the actual thought processes with which decisions were made. It manifested itself in such a way that society would have an improved standard of living, overflowing with abundance and prosperity such as the world had never witnessed. The revolution brought about a transformation from the unsophisticated village livelihood to the modern day technological society. New forms of transportation, communication and systematic management was revolutionized and brought into the public eye. For example railway, steamboat and telegraph were the inventions that came into existence because of the advancement in technology. The next paragraph will allow you to see the factors that contributed to the industrial revolution within the United States.

The industrial revolution in the United States commenced in the textile industries and spread to the other industries. What led to the United States industrial growth? To answer this question, it should be noted that the availability of capital, economic, social, thrift and the political aspects all play major roles in the shaping of this new society which was persuaded to be gainfully employed, save money, invent and compete. Factors of production including land, labor, capital, and entrepreneurship were abundantly available in the United States. Employees were literate and able to have technical manuals available to them, which maximized productivity, performance and efficiency in the factory. Early American society's forefathers were actively interested in economic expansion and industrialization of the United States and thus participated financially and expressively. An important question that may perhaps arise may concern the factors that critically contributed to the advancement of industrialization in United States? The corresponding answer to that question would be the availability of capital, machines, technology and intellectual individuals.

Samuel Slater immigrated to United States from Britain and with him was brought his technical knowledge. He developed the mechanized spinning process and created the first textile mill in the United States. The inventors never had any recess, as they were very busy perfecting invention upon invention of which many escalated into major inventions. There were several textile industries constructed from coast to coast in the United States. With a global population of over six billion, and the wide variety of tastes, styles and cultures, the clothing industry which had existed for hundreds, if not thousands of years, would continue to grow and evolve, and now at an alarming rate due to these remarkable inventions. It may be noted that is one were only to traveled globally it can be seen that every nation has been impacted by textile industry in one way or another, especially with arrival of mass production. With mass production, the textile industry was now capable of producing large quantities of casual, professional, summer, spring and winter clothes; indeed a piece of clothing for every taste imaginable. It should be noted that while many of us have these types of clothes hanging in our closets we should not forget that our forerunner suffered at the hands of trial and error, performed arduous work with their bare hands, and created these inventions for the betterment of human beings.

The customs of textile production before industrial revolution included production of quality handicrafts. Although there were no mechanical devices available, people were resourceful enough to use their bare hands to produce quality attire. Before industrial revolution the weavers, combers, bleachers, dyers worked in their home. Thus, people endured the onerous task of weaving from the raw material to finished product. In the next paragraph one will see how business was managed prior to industrialization. Let us now consider the business management issues that had to be considered. What were the business management concepts prior to industrialization? An autocratic process or the concept of boss imposing control on the employees governed the traditional management thought. However, as poignant as this may sound, it was a learning process in the past era. At one point it was believed that discipline, corporal punishment and fines were the primary motivator for employees to work. The system of management before the advent of modern management was in essence micromanagement.

During the medieval era, which had its own system of management, the businesses were managed under the guild system. The guild management had inspectors that inspected employees' finished products to maintain quality, and had seminars that trained employees to increase their productive capabilities. The guild was supportive of a code of ordinance. Employees were given promotional incentives to enhance their morale, quality assurance benchmark and employee performance evaluations to improve performance. These organizations had plans and objectives and utilize policies and procedures to accomplish them. Managerial personnel in general have an affirmative duty to maintain and encourage the employees to comply with business policies and procedures. The managerial system that was crafted during medieval era had absolutely endured the test of time and continues to develop even to the present day.

The organization that was created prior to industrial revolution was popularly known as weaving guild: it was customary for households to spin wool into yarn, while weavers were responsible for weaving yarn into cloth in shops owned by master weavers. The master weavers were entrepreneurs who owned the business, managed weaver's productivity, and stressed conformance to standard, conduct, product quality and performance review before the item was sold to consumers. A management function in an organization includes responsibilities to crosscheck subordinates daily work performance and to produce results that would benefit both employees and the organization. The management, organization and society have goals and objectives that must be realized. The objective of an organization is to make profit. The goals and objectives of families, communities and society are quite similar, as they would like to satisfy the need for livelihood and survival.

There are many notable pioneers of management thought, but the passage will focus on one of those that affected factory operation. Without further ado, one will be able to verify the identity of the pioneers. Max Weber was the individual who initiated the management concept of bureaucracy; he went on to categorize it as the paramount and realistic management thought that would give the advantage to a conglomerate organization. Moreover, Frederick Taylor was the person who established scientific management, which included worker efficiency; lunch breaks and variable pay policy. Thus, organizations that implemented the concept of scientific management saw the reality of immense productivity and employees' satisfaction.

The modern organizations derived it's tenets of job

requirements of managers, mode of operations of managers, and the job description of management from industrial revolution. Having said that let us look closely into industrial growth and systematic management. One will now see what was responsible for the development of industrial growth and systematic management. First, what led to the development of industrial growth? The continuous-process manufacturing fueled the development of industrial growth. The inventor of the continuous-process manufacturing was popularly known as Oliver Evans of Delaware.

The organization that implemented continuous-process manufacturing experienced substantive productivity and abundant revenue. Thus, several industries in the United States began to use this production system and it eventually led to massive industrial growth. This is a question that one might probably ask. What are the forces that were responsible for the development of industrial growth? The adequate answer is to say that the invention of railroads, which was motorized by steam engines, which led to a transportation revolution; and the advent of telegraph and the transatlantic cable that brought about a communication revolution. The circumstances that contributed to the development of systematic management were attributed to the act of performance assessment, cost cutting measures, delegation of authority and responsibility to subordinate and continuous improvement. Thus, among the many benefits that will accrue to the organization that are well grounded in systematic management include low cost products and competitive advantages.

The essential functions of a manager comprise oversight, coordination, and supervision of the work of assigned staff, review of projects, problem solving, preparation of policies and procedures and compliance reviews. There were several problems encountered during the early period of the factories system, thus, there are clear evidence that there were substantial dilemmas in the factories during industrial revolution. Several researchers had strategically developed systems to resolve these problems to no avail, until management implemented scientific management. Positive outcomes materialized in the factories and the dawn of reduction in cost of manufacturing was seen.

An abundance of textile products is now available all over the world, though the industry had a humble beginning. Varieties of clothes worn today are a significant testament that the revolution effect on textile industry was authentic. The technical advancement of steam power decreased the cost of manufacturing, product prices and as a result produced market expansion. In earlier times, members of society worked at home with family members and their daily routine included spinning yarn and weaving cloth. Producing cloth was not an easy task but in the 18th-century Great Britain innovators developed several technical apparatus that eased manual labor of home workers. John Kay was the inventor of the flying shuttle and it was in the year 1733 that the world witnessed this ingenious invention, which mechanized the operation of weaving. The characteristics of technology in the textile industry brought the benefit of an assembly line with mass production, large capacity output, standardized production made at lower per unit cost and finished products anticipated for a mass market.

The management of several industries including textile industry realized early on that customer satisfaction was very important and because of this, had begun producing quality attire, with the assumption that this is merely an exchange for the money the consumers pay for the clothing. Each consumer was an individual with needs that varied from city to city and household to household. The industrial revolution had transformed the textile industry on a global scale. This era was actually the time when invention of technological developments had radically been manifested to drive management, production, organization and economic growth. Thereafter, it led to the increase in the standards of performance of industries. The advent of rapid inventions, innovations and creativity eventually delivered modernization of organization to society.

James Hargreaves invented the spinning jenny machine, Richard Arkwright invented water-powered spinning machine and Samuel Crompton discovered the mule machine. Eventually, the new system of manufacturing cloth was developed after many discoveries and improvements of machines. Let us now look into the steam engine, which would be categorized as the catalyst that spearheaded the industrial revolution. We have substantial evidence that Watt made his greatest technological break-through when he transformed the up-and-down motion of the drive beam into the rotary motion of an engine. This led to a host of new utilizations for steam power; for example, lifting coal and ore from mines, supplying power for breweries and oil mills, and eventually powering railway locomotives and steamships.

The steam engine was the catalyst that caused the paradigm shift in the industrial system. What is the definition of a steam engine? A steam engine is an external combustion heat engine that utilized the thermal energy that exists in steam, converting it to mechanical work. The contribution of the steam engine in the factory system was stupendous because it was used to power the mechanical apparatus that were responsible in producing finish goods. The textile industry and society witnessed the advancement in the technology, which cultivated a better economy, a better standard of living, full employment, higher salary and net income. The civilization of this period depicted systematic progress in the communities, for instance, people were commuting from their home to work in ever increasing factory workplaces. They were no longer engaged in home employment and handicraft systems of making yarn were eradicated. The textile industry started using steam engine machines to mass-produce its products.

Our predecessors were pioneers as they created many inventions, which benefited several industries including the textile industry. In order to distribute textile products from coast to coast in the U.S., canals and roads were constructed primarily for the purpose of transporting raw materials, cloth, consignments, inventories and marketing products. The industrialists knew that finished products, raw material, food and society would appreciate reliable, faster and less costly forms of transportation. Thus, transportation like steamboats, railways and trucks became faster and shipped large amounts of manufactured goods from coast to coast.

Communication technology also allowed the textile industry to engage in a network association between raw material suppliers, producers, distributors and consumers. In addition, the advent of transportation and communication technology benefited the textile industry, because the textile industry was able to produce cloth in large batch volume production, use continuous processing, and sell cloth in a volume distribution and mass market. The inventors created new manufacturing machinery so that the work process was changed from the home to factories and the demography was rapidly increasing. The textile industry was productive because the tools in the factory were technically enhanced. The technically advanced machines brought about the mass production of textile products. As one can verify, there were many hand held tools that helped enhance the textiles industry in this period. There were many advantages attributed to these inventions, for example, the changes permitted a worker to produce more. A single spinner or weaver produced volumes of yarn or cloth. Hence, the industrial revolution was known as a landmark because it brought higher productivity and economic prosperity.

The benefits of having factories during the revolution were several, but the significant advantage was that it provided transformation of the families, communities, society, organizational operation and the management procedures. There was an availability of the first generation of computer that provided the needed operational efficiency coupled with mass production and the increased revenue that accrued to the benefit of textile industry. The textile industry could boast of efficient operations because the apparatus and computer systems contributed vastly to its operations. This technology was not everything though because the organizations needed capable managers. The majority of the employees also needed the skills to work with the modern gadgets, therefore training and seminars needed to be provided. Let us look into the problems and perspectives of management during the industrial revolution.

The era of industrial revolution brought about ingenuity in management and as a matter of fact the new management styles affected transportation, communication, mining, textiles and other industries. It was apparent that employees at the factories were laggard, unproductive, incompetent, inexperienced and insubordinate to the management. The industry's situation yearned for experienced managers because management schools were non-existent. We have information that with substantial evidence that during the industrial revolution there were managerial problems.

In describing these problems, he referred to the technology, labor relations, supply, marketing channels, finances, human resources and especially applicants that possessed mechanic skills. He revealed that if employees with dissimilar work skills were assembled to work in close proximity to each other there would be unity, diversity and issues resolved. In the factory settings the dilemma of working condition were deplorable, employees were working sixteen hours in a day, employees were underpaid, women were exploited, underemployed and mistreated.

He also demonstrated with cogent evidence that the problems during the industrial revolution included job monotony, boredom and management found the amicable solution through the implementation of the division of labor. Furthermore, he concluded that the theory of division of labor was responsible for the high productivity in the factory systems. In the perspective of management during industrial revolution, the management was persuaded with the concept of micromanagement of a workforce would help produce efficiency and maximum productivity. Therefore employees were subjected to rigorous supervision, regimentation and discipline.

It is interesting to note that the industrialist implemented several activities to overcome the encumbrances, for instance, workers lack of experience, education, literacy and training by means of lectures and paradigm. Training was conducted largely by oral instruction, demonstration, and trial and error. The hierarchy in companies glorified the principles of organizational efficiency, mass production, employee satisfaction and motivation. The principles of the modern management should not be taken lightly because of the fact that our predecessors paid so dearly for these concepts that are now so common in our today's organization. Now that thoughtful awareness of the industrial revolution is achieved, let us now peruse the textile industry and other industries on era of second industrial revolution.

Where can they find a proficient manager? There is a need for efficient employees. There is also a need for management who is proficient in responsibilities of training textile employees and work of his/her subordinate and micro managing the technical devices. The factories needed proficient managers that would empower employees in order to seek out solutions to operational problems. In fact economic theory identified that the entrepreneurs/managers performed a discrete role in combining the traditional three factors of production in the ever-growing factory system. With size came the need for managers, the need for a capable, disciplined, trained, motivated workforce, and the need for implementing the planning, organizing, and controlling of operations in the early enterprise.

Micromanaging is the act of managing employees with extreme control. During the era of industrial revolution, it was noted that several organizations instituted micromanagement forms of controlling employees and their structures lacked delegation of responsibilities. Ideally, employees were empowered and capable decision-makers. The caveat with micromanagement structure included discouraging people's empowerment. Thus, factory workers were confronted with strict rules, close supervision by managers, and overseers. The clock ruled life in the mills. At times our modern day management may get so overwhelmed with everyday production numbers and meetings that they tend to forget about who works for them. Management should realize that a little bit of employee recognition could go a long way in improving employees' self-esteem. Management should make employees feel appreciated and happy. Thereafter employees will turn around and deliver that same gratitude in their work and customer service.

The second industrial revolution has absolutely urbanized the global society; it arrived and brought the chemical, electrical, petroleum and steel industries. In addition, mass manufacturing of consumer goods created full employment for the ever-increasing society and people were entertained with goods like cinema, radio and gramophone. The epoch of the second industrial revolution brought about civilization and it certainly enhanced several industrial expansions as well as the textiles industry.

There were numerous escalations of companies that grew at a greater rate than the economy as a whole and usually directed a relatively high proportion of income back into the society and business. When the second industrial revolution materialized people knew what caused it. They knew it because the vast manufacturing technology spread to new industries. The second phase of industrial revolution manifested because of the contribution of the technological advances, improved management, commerce, market, population, high income, modern transportation and communication progress. In addition, the development of industrial growth contributed massively to the standard of living in America and all over the world. Carnegie was the man who advocated for and successfully combined technology and management to provide more jobs, reduce prices, expand markets and advance industrial development.

Overall, it seemed that the second industrial revolution that appeared in United States was profound to the fact that United States became a world superpower in the realms of manufacturing and productivity. Furthermore, in a sense, another contributory factor to industrial growth included production continuous-method and American system of interchangeable parts. For example, the automobile industry depicted a reality that whenever manufacturers combine continuous-methods and American systems there would be great effects of mass production.

Henry Ford was the person that innovatively mass-produced motor parts in order to produce automobile. This mass production system and scientific management eventually depicted United States as the number one industrial nation in the world.

We have perused the textiles industry procedures and modes of operations before, during and after the industrial revolution and we have also witnessed the effect of this revolution on other industries. We explored the benefits of this period in terms of technological advancements and how they were integrated into the textiles business and other organizations. Although there were many obstacles that were confronted by members of the industry, solutions and remedies were presented to overcome them by trial and error as well as other methods. All these were possible because of the persistence of the motivated innovators, inventors and management pioneers alike. Overall, it can now be seen how the industrial revolution radically changed society on a globally scale.

CHAPTER 4
How Corporate America attain Revenue growth

The main ideology behind this strategy is to stand out among the crowd and say that we are different, we are better and we are going to serve the need of yours like no other company can does. Without having a competitive advantage it's quite impossible now days to compete or even survive in the market. To gain competitive advantages which will differentiate a company from its competitor approaches needs to be carefully planned and strategically sound. The three strategic approaches that will be discussed here is differentiation, cost leadership and response. In this strategy, as the name says, the company must differentiate its product or services from its competitor's product or services.

If the product that are available on the market are of the same type and does the same benefits, consumers will get confused and might end up buying competitors product. To avoid such situation, company needs to strategically differentiate the products with its competitors. Secondly, the product needs to be better than its competitors product in terms of may be quality so that the company can give a reason to its customer to but its product and on the other hand the customers get more benefited so that in the future they select this particular company's product. The main ideology behind this strategy is to stand out among the crowd and say that we are different, we are better and we are going to serve the need of yours like no other company can does. The second important strategy that a company can follow in order to gain competitive advantage is the cost leadership. What this strategy does, is to simply offer the product to its customer at the cheapest possible rate. However, this strategy does not say to supply the product below the cost of its production, but instead it suggests cutting the unnecessary cost in a way so that the company can offer the cheapest.

In today's world, people spend every single penny very carefully and if they are attracted by even very little discount. This is the advantage that this strategy helps to take by both producing and selling mass amount at the same time or cutting the cost as much as possible so that it can offer the cheapest rate. This strategy suggests prioritizing the customer at the first and then rest of the others. In today's world, every company is customer oriented and most of them try its best to consistently focus on its customers. The company which loses the attention fails to survive or loses its customers. On the other hand, the company which can focus without being distracted and response to its customers at the earliest wins the heart of the customers and increases sales. Additional to the fact, that the company is gaining a customer, because of continuous focus and rapid response, the company does not let the customer think of the other competitors or other products. This strategy increases the popularity of company's customer service and thus helps the company to gain positive word-of-mouth through its customers.

Time-based competition is a source of competitive advantage which is gained by a company through utilizing the time to the fullest in every aspect of its business. If a company can master the technique of time-based competition, it will save time and money on every phases of its business and thus will gain the first mover benefits. To become a time-based competitor a firm needs to accomplish few tasks such as, people within the companies having clear understanding on the rules and responsibilities, making the value-delivery system flexible and implementing such time-based strategy that actually surprises its customers. To implement such strategy, the firm needs to perform a complete process analysis to understand the current operations of the business. The company needs to develop different measurement system that emphasizes more on time. By forming various cross-functional teams and engineering methods, the company can speed up the new product introduction and as well as regular production time. Different managerial decisions need to be evaluated to check whether decisions are appropriate in terms of time. Some methods such as JIT (Just in Time) needs to be adopted to avoid storage cost and possible delays. Division of labor is another approach that can be adopted to set up the best skilled people to do the right kind of works. Last but not the least, reward system can be adopted where employees will be rewarded based on their performance and activity yet producing the product of the finest quality. Because of adopting all these techniques, Corporate America can out run its competitors through offering its better quality product at a faster speed.

We all have some idea what product and services are. But defining product and services from the operation management view is way more different and specific at the same time. There are some specific criteria that the products or services must meet in order to be counted as a product or service from operation management angle. Some of those criteria's are given below for both products and services. Operation management firstly defines its products by its functions. It also refers to the features that the product shows and how it meets the demand of the customer. Also when the product is designed to be manufactured in the future, the design specifies all its specifications and capabilities. Unless and until the design does not shows the specification meeting the expectation of the firm and the clients, the designed cannot be passed. An engineering drawing is a pre-requisite to any product and its manufacturing phase in its life cycle.

The engineering drawing is drawn with high care and its shows all the accurate specification of the product. The drawing also discloses the dimension of the product, level of tolerance and the materials that will be used to build the product. The technology that will be used in case of building the product is also specified in the drawing section. Last but not the least is the bill of material for the product which is also a prerequisite for any product. The bill of material typically includes all the necessary equipment and materials needed to build the product, the list of the components needed and also specifies the quantity needed. In the product structure section the plant and the series of work is also specified. Other than this, few other documents such as assembly chart, route sheet, work order etc. documents are also needed to ensure the best quality and most optimized use of resources for the product. In terms of services, the focus is mainly on the customer interaction part of the service rather than the production of any materials that come along the path. For every service there needs to be a service design which includes the level of customer participation in the design, level of customer participation in the delivery process and the participation level in both design and delivery process.

One crucial phase of the service is when the customer meets the service which is also known as the moment of truth. Moment of truth is the time when the customer satisfaction level is determined. This is the moment when the firm usually gains its business or loses it. In the documentation part for the service, a document includes the high level of customer interaction necessities, explicit job instruction for the moment of truth. It also includes the scripts, story boards and other techniques required to get the job done perfectly. In simple words, success of the service depends on the satisfaction level of its customers. So, to be a model service according to operation management, every service needs to be well organized and the people need to be prepared and responsible for each and every action. Service is more revenue oriented and the location strategy of the service has some important impact on the business as a convenient location ensures better customer contact and also increases the volume of business. On the other hand, Production Company's location strategy largely affects the cost of production. Better location strategy helps the company to minimize the production cost and thus offer the product at the cheapest price possible. In simple words, a service company sets up their location in a way so that they can establish more and more connection with the customers and thus generate even more revenue, on the other hand, production companies set up business in a way so that they can minimize the cost of transporting goods and raw materials. Location strategy is extremely important regardless of the fact whether it is a service or manufacturing company. Different location strategy is adopted by a service and a manufacturing company because both the business does not equally focus on customer and the goods. Service location strategy is quite different from manufacturing company's location strategy and the reasons behind them are given below. Companies that operates globally needs to follow certain strategies that helps them to compete with its product in the foreign market. To begin such operation, companies need to do a research on the foreign market to analyze the demand and the market trend of the industry that they are going to operate in. Even after choosing the foreign market carefully, while in operation the company needs to follow some strategies that allow them to operate and survive in the market. The four basic strategies that most of the companies follow is the licensing of the product, standardization of the product, economies of scale and cross-cultural learning. This strategy is followed by the global companies to maintain proper authorization while working the foreign market. In case of import/export in abroad countries such documents are mandatory in order to operate the business smoothly and avoid all the restriction that can be imposed by the foreign governments. Franchising can be also be an strategy that falls under this category where a company can operate in the foreign market while still using a trusted company name and ensuring the same quality of the product.

When a company adopts such strategy is reduces the risk of operating only in the domestic market where a sudden change in the economy might bring the company down. For example, if a country faces economic down turn and at that time all the companies that will be operating only in the market are expected to face loss or slower business. On the other hand, if the company operates in other foreign market at that time, it has some chances to regain control over its business and tackle all the financial boundaries. Standardization is the process of offering products that are of high quality and uses the latest technologies. Standardized product helps a company to maximize compatibility, interoperability, safety, repeatability. It can also facilitate the company with commoditization of formerly custom processes. In today's world, people are fond of technologies and innovations. To acquire that market, a company that is operating globally needs to standardize its product, increase the quality and life time of the product and thus gain competitive advantage to stand out among the rival companies.

Economies of scale generally refer to the process in which a company can gain cost advantages over its competitors. To be more specific, because of this strategy the company can produce each of the additional out-put unit at a lower cost and thus offer its product to the customers at the cheapest price. When a company gains cost advantage, its product certainly becomes more affordable for the customers and when they does a cost vs. benefit analysis, the product seems to be even more considerable. Additional to this fact, if a company achieves the economies of scale, it can certainly reduce the cost per item and rule out all the unnecessary cost that adds up and increases the cost of the product eventually. This sort of competitive advantage is a must to become the best seller in the market. Most of the time, to achieve economies of scale, companies needs to produce items in bulk and go for a mass distribution.

No two human are of the same type. This statement gets even truer when people of different country are brought into consideration. Culture, behavior, demand, expectation etc. varies from country to country and thus it is extremely important for a company to know the culture and other human activities of the market that it is going to operate in. Without knowing the expectation of the people of a foreign country, it is impossible to understand their needs what sort of products will attract those market. Failure to understand these cross cultural factors might even impact the growth of the business. Other than human, there are other factors as well that the company need to bear in mind in terms of foreign investment. An example might be the weather. A place where it is sunny 90% of the time might not be the best place to sell umbrellas.

The online business owners are absolutely convinced that if companies want to obtain a spontaneous response from the email promotion of the prospective customers, the inclusion of the key words such as, free trial, sample, product, discount and limited time offers will activate rapid responses. Incentives should prompt customers to revisit the Web site. For instance, the authentic incentives that will satisfy customers include online club membership, product customization and personalized gifts. Concurrently, sales promotion is a paramount ingredient to elicit urgent procurement of products or services. Meanwhile, the tenet of advertising gives consumers reasons to buy products while sales promotions confer an incentive to procure products.

The online companies are currently seizing the majority of these incentive tools for product promotion, for instance, these incentive tools are offer to consumers: (a) samples, (b) coupons, (c) cash refund, (d) offers, and (e) prices off. In addition, other incentive tools offer are: (a) premium, (b) prices, (c) patronage rewards, (d) free trials, (e) warranties, (f) tie-in promotion price off, (g) cross promotion, (h) point-of-purchase display, (i) demonstration; trade promotion and business and sale-force promotions. Upper management is now an ardent proponent of promotions as an effective sales tool and customers' incentive program. Consequently, to make the incentive program an effective marketing campaign, the online business owner should consider incorporating individualized incentive allocation. Simultaneously, companies should establish a policy regarding customer incentive programs and recognition awards. The policy should recognize and acknowledge exemplary customers.

Companies should allocate incentives such as free products to the prospective customers in the identified areas. In addition, incentives or awards are appropriate when company allocate it for at least four times a year with the award period defined by the executive manager of the company. However, Customers have supremacy; they are always right and are the final arbiter of business decisions. In effective email marketing campaign, online corporation shall acquire, and retain consumers to promote and ensure success in reducing attrition rate of customers.

The concept of Web-based electronic commerce mentioned that the Internet technology began in 1996 from that time people demanded to know about consumer behavior concerning the use of the Web for commerce. The higher the sales of merchandise when a company utilizes old fashion catalog, the higher the indication of sales and revenue when the company adopts the Web-based electronic commerce. When consumers prefer shopping on a global scale an entrepreneur needs to seize the advantage via electronic commerce.

E-commerce model has changed the business because the function represents the potential revenue and non-revenue. Thus, the cogent monetary results included revenue that are increased because of the capacity growth and price differentiation, cost that are minimized because of the clever-way of reducing cost of good and operating cost, and minimization of asset carrying cost because of the management of the cost of working capital and/or fixed asset. However, the non-revenue that creates value may include a variety of visible or invisible results that may materialized because of the e-commerce implementation, for instance, products and services continuous quality improvement, short and quick product delivery schedule, state of the art customer satisfaction, worldwide extension of products services and information, availability and permanency of information. Ingredient such as value proposition model, value-added e-commerce offering supporting resources, revenue model, cost models and value creation could be utilized to craft a new e-commerce model and improve on current e-commerce models. Narrated ingredients are indispensable for developing well-organized e-commerce business models that will satisfy purchaser's aspiration, to cause higher business performance and to maintain organizational competitive edge via e-commerce.

Society knows that jobs are changing. They are impacted by ongoing workplace changes, new technologies, and are rapidly becoming more knowledge based. To keep up will require continuous learning on employee part - an investment both on and off the job. Since training and development is a shared responsibility for both worker and the employer, organization commitment is to provide employee with lifelong learning opportunities. For example my organization offer intranet courses in Technology, Business Management, Safety and Technical training. Organization that implements this aspect of training can help workforce increase value, versatility, and career potential. Job performance and job satisfaction will improve. And, employee will be better able to achieve personal and career goals.

Improving the performance of organization is a major part of employees' job. One should know that it is a difficult task to focus on in the midst of change, resource constraints, and uncertainty. Employee training can do a lot to identify the key business goals and challenges, and then prescribe specific learning activities to help achieve those goals. However, research on leading edge organizations and today's workforce reveals two things one should know. First, investing in the development of a professional, versatile workforce is the best defense against changing and uncertain times. And second, employees today know the work environment is changing and expect to be trained and kept current by their employer.

In Corporate America, several managers are known to introduce new products and services which will enhance the living standard of people and boost revenue growth of the organizations. Several managers have innovative concepts and new idea to enable them to develop newer and better goods and services for the organizations. The managers should discuss open ideas that can be translated into products and services. The director should stop planning and working on any projects which will waste their time and energy. The managers must erect safeguards against risks that may cause financial wastage of the organizations and business failure. The sales representatives must understand the needs of the customers and efficiently presents the products and services to them. The sales representatives must understand sales promotions, how to increase sales techniques and offer the products and services in the proper way. The managers must influence the target markets in order for them to have hunger and thus request for the products and services. The management must create new venues and provide new markets for the products and services. The sales representatives must increase sales and add new markets daily. The managers will enhance the organizations' ability to grow and in turn make profit. Attracting new customers to an existing products or persuading existing customers to buy more of it also can create substantial revenue growth. The managers should boost revenue growth by introducing new product categories, new markets, gain markets, price changes, overall expansion, mergers, and acquisitions activities.

In Corporate America, e-commerce organizations are cognizant of the global market and its limitless opportunities. These organizations should benefit from cost effectiveness, lower fixed cost and profitability in global environment. The products of e-commerce organizations are not enough to meet the need of seven billion people in the world. The internet has seen extraordinary expansion in the United States and is now spreading across Asia. Consumers can now see millions of products on e-commerce web sites. The customer point of reference is imperative for global expansion. The internet and e-commerce are responsible for quicker communication, transportation, and financial streams; the world is getting smaller. For example, products developed in one country, such as Gucci purses, Mont Blanc pens, McDonald's hamburgers, Japanese sushi, Chanel suits; German BMWs becoming popular in other countries.

Consumers are excited about buying merchandise online, so there are more prospective customers for global e-commerce organizations. These organizations should be grateful that people in a particular nation may be more willing to buy online. The global e-commerce organizations should comprehend the factors influencing national differences in consumer acceptance of e-commerce purchasing.

Organizations that have information technology resources in place are more likely to adopt and execute e-commerce. Circumstances often influence corporations to venture into global business environment. Scholars have determined that global companies offer excellent products and bargain prices. Various companies may go global in order to prevent their competitors from cutting into their home markets. The global marketing is predicated on both information technology and the customer.

The expansion of smaller organizations into global the global environment, though excellent adventure, but the large organizations will suffer from erosion of their domestic market. Small organizations that offer global products and that have low production costs have an advantage over larger organizations. The movement towards market fragmentation will escalate, and large organizations will need to respond accordingly. The global e-commerce environment will witness increasing numbers of customers, suppliers and prospective alliance partners. The management of organizations will find it imperative to understand which the new global e-commerce ventures work.

In order to probe the target customers, this study will use the survey research method and questionnaires. Survey questionnaires are instruments that the research participants are required to complete. The survey method can entail questionnaires and personal interviews. The e-commerce web sites and e-mail systems will be used to administer the questionnaires to prospective consumers. The managements of small or medium-sized enterprises are likely to seek understanding of the target market. The purposes of this book are to make the domestic operations global and localizing the organizational web site. The researcher will collect the data from respondents who are prospective global customers. As a caveat, the global respondents may not be entirely ethical and truthful. With advanced communication technology, the e-commerce companies are in a favorable position to receive information from global customers.

In this book, the researcher subscribed to Zoomerang

and used its web site to distribute the survey questionnaires. Online surveys typically can be administrated more cost effectively than traditional mail or telephone surveys. E-commerce organizations can use online research companies to conduct surveys or to create and administer their own. For instance, survey sites such as Zoomerang.com allow organizations to use, edit, and distribute survey templates to Zoomerang's panel of consumers. Market research consists of collecting data that will help an organization identify prospective products and customers. There are two general kinds of market research. Primary research involves collecting first-hand information using surveys, personal interviews, and focus groups. This kind of research is usually used to elicit feedback on brands, products, or new marketing operations on topics that have not been previously studied. Secondary research depends on published information for market analysis. Both primary and secondary research can be conducted online less expensively, and often more accurately than offline.

Academic researchers usually study quantitative and qualitative data. Quantitative data can be conveyed as percentages or other numbers. Researchers analyze quantitative data by using statistical software that identifies relationships between certain variable, or by studying factors that affect how someone. Several researchers use survey questions to elicit qualitative responses. Several researchers analyze qualitative responses by grouping responses into similar sub-segments based on the answers given. Content analysis is a mean of identifying the major categories of responses.

In this book, the survey methodology may be prone to limitations, because participants may come to the research with biases and prejudices that may diminish the objectivity of the survey to appear knowledgeable and in a positive light. The researchers may not be able to avoid social desirability in a survey because respondents do not like to answer sensitive or embarrassing questions. Such questions may be problematic in a face-to-face or a phone interview. Another limitation is that researchers may not be able to ascertain that the person to whom a survey was mailed (e.g. the head of a household or the head of a company) was the person who actually completed it. On the phone, the researchers may be speaking people who lie about their identity. Conversely, with personal interviews, the researchers know the interviewees in a way that they cannot with mail surveys or phone interviews. The personal interviews allow researchers to collect more detailed information. Researchers may use personal interviews on their second phase of research following an initial survey. Several researchers prefer to use deep interviews with a target segment in order to arrive at more precise answers to issues and questions brought up in the survey research. Other shortcomings are the excessive amount of time spent on gathering information and the low response rate; it is also more difficult to persuade someone to complete an extended interview than to take a short survey.

Focus groups, like personal interviews, allow researchers to collect more precise responses to questions and to probe issues. The drawback is that focus groups are often less structured so that participants can express themselves. Focus groups often comprise 8 to 12 people. The facilitator often encourages the members to discuss their viewpoints and preferences. The participants log into a chat room, where they express their opinions and ideas and online focus groups usually last one hour. The advantage of focus groups is that several views and opinions can be learned in a short period of time. Academic researchers are notorious for vilifying the focus group method, claiming that more extroverted people tend to dominate the discussion. This is less of a problem online because participants cannot observe each other and are more confident expressing themselves by typing.

Observation is another method of market research. The researcher may watch consumers as they buy products. Online customer tracking is the same as observation. Customer tracking includes observing consumers as they navigate a web site and weigh its offerings. Global e-commerce organizations may use cookies to collect data on consumer preferences, dislikes, challenges and satisfaction in order to improve future visits to the site. The best ways to send a universal corporate message to the global audience are through e-mail, blogs and the web site. The managers of e-commerce organizations are responsible for using these conduits to persuade prospective customers to purchase products. The managers should provide continuous follow-up communication to assist the company in enhancing its products, services, brand image and maximizing sales. Small or medium-sized companies have expanded business model to the internet in order to obtain vast market coverage and greater global market share and profitability.

The only outstanding challenge for non-English users of the internet is the dominance of the English language. The World Wide Web and Arabic browsers have partially solved the problem of orthography, but text-based areas such as e-mail remain problematic. Conversely, managers of e-commerce corporations should integrate cultural orientation of the people from African, Europe, Asian, Middle East and South America in the organization's web sites during initial stages of the e-commerce global expansion. Accordingly, small or medium-sized enterprises are more knowledgeable of cultural diversity. A corporation hoping to operate in a global environment needs to speak the language and, understand the customs, culture and interests of their target customers. Reebok.com web site has specific sites for the United Kingdom and France. The manager is responsible for displaying the Reebok brand name on all the web sites, but the specific products and promotions that they depict differ from country to country. E-commerce organizations may benefit from targeting global customers. In global e-commerce, management should accommodate cultural differences when implementing a global marketing strategy. Some organizations might not want to take their operations global if their market is large enough. Managers would not need to learn other languages and laws and handle volatile currencies and political and legal uncertainties. Conversely, when international business is the option, managers will be encouraged to accommodate global customers' needs.

The managers should ascertain that the corporate web sites are globalized, localized and monetized for a worldwide audience. The web is a global medium, but several sites do nothing for worldwide nations and global audiences. People from global environment can visit a site, but they will regret if language, cultural, and economic transactional issues are not manipulated well. Internationalization and localization of e-commerce are becoming an increasingly imperative factor as web sites start crossing national boundary. Globalization and localization vary from simple concerns, such as how information like a phone number is meaningfully represented, to severe concerns, such as political and religious beliefs. Internationalization refers to the software changes required to sustain diverse languages, dates and times, currencies, weights and measures, and number formats. Localization can be defined as the method of recreating the human-computer interface and translating content of the web site to support a local culture. The web site genres can be implemented for a global audience. The genres pattern offer the underpinning for creating sites that are localized to diverse audiences on a global scale. For example, the content of the Yahoo.com web site in United States carry English language while Yahoo.com in Taiwan integrates the language of Taiwan. The objective of this book is to expand domestic operations to a global audience by localizing corporate web site. The objective is to make the web site carry the contents in language of the country in which it appears. When the leader of a global corporation opens warehouses around the world, he or she may have to hire local. The translators' responsibility includes using different languages specific to individual nation to write the web contents, products, pop-up advertisement and other commercials

In this book, the corporate warehouses will need to be situated in strategic locations around the world to reduce the cost of shipping and accelerate delivery of products to customers. In this book, the global e-commerce corporation will have web sites transacting business in fifteen countries in Europe, Asia, Africa, and South America. The e-commerce manager will incorporate local pattern like (shopping cart, quick-flow checkout, dates, times, currencies, taxes, addresses, and shipping conditions) into the web sites for global customers. This includes ensuring global customers to see their own country privacy laws, fair information practices, and privacy policy on the e-commerce global web sites. The web site will not include terms and concepts that may not be widely recognized in global setting. Terms like 1RS and ESPN may be common to people in the United States, but they are not as recognizable in other nations of the world. In fact, most acronyms, excluding the most global ones, such as SCIJBA, will not be known. Things like government agencies, government policies, and local laws and practices often have different names and interpretation in other nations.

In order to implement global business operations, the manager performed and prepared the web site flow charts; hired translators; incorporated local language-driven web contents; tested the site and launched web sites in host countries. In addition, the manager implemented the blueprint for localizing the web site; incorporated the culture of the country into the web site; and integrated the marketing logistics (Feng & Yuan 2007). Organizations engaged in global operation face major changes in transporting their products. The prompt development of the door-to-door mode of transportation will help the organizations to meet the needs of consumers' pressing demand for the products. Several global organizations prefer to collaborate with global logistics service providers in order to adapt easily to changes in the global environment (Feng & Yuan 2007).

In this book, developing localization by redesigning the human-computer interface on the web site and converting content to support global local culture will be the main performance. Localization is the procedure of recreating the human simultaneously with computer interface and translating content to support a local culture. In this book, embedding globalization into a web site during initial site design is the priority and then localizing for global audiences on the basis of need. I discovered that most sites are not initially designed with a global audience in mind, they are not often easily localized when the time comes. The management of e-commerce corporations should join global partnership of companies in order to benefit from global distribution of their products and global procurement. Global logistics management (GLM) will help e-commerce global organizations to reduce the following: (a) operation cost, (b) pressure of inventory, and (c) financial risk. GLM incorporates superior production situations on a global scale, using advanced information and communication technologies as well as efficient information flow.

Centralized localization management offers translation services to the entire web site teams, but does not frequently have the domain expertise of each of the regions. Decentralized localization management has domain knowledgeable individuals spread all over the organization. The decentralized localization may be deficient in the localization of corporation in order to assist manage the process most effectively. It is difficult to attain consistency with decentralized teams because they may not know what other teams around the world are doing. The manager in this study will assess the capabilities of the organization's resources and financial investment to decide what strategy works best. In this book, a mix approach will be utilized, using some characteristics of centralized management, along with local expertise, is the best resolution.

The manager in this study will be cognizant of local customs regarding the color of the web sites. For example, sites steered toward China or Taiwan should be cautious of how white is used. The global customers from China or Taiwan will regard white color as the emblem of mourning. Colors, images, and icons that have one meaning in one cultural environment may be unpleasant in another. As a caveat, the manager in this book will take the time to comprehend the value of specific color choices and icons. "In some cases those colors and icons add value to the brand identity and add a local feel. There will be an acceptable balance between global structure and local appeal.

In this book, all the global teams are cognizant that in several nations people may use mobile device to navigate web sites. The site will be created to be reachable from mobile devices as they become popular in new environments. The page explanation format for mobile devices may not be similar from country to country. The webmaster will obtain gateways in order to enhance the corporation web site in the global local markets. A nation may prefer WAP devices while the other nation may like to use HDMI. Accordingly, in global environment, instant messaging protocols are mostly the preference. In this book, site managers will implement gateways to these protocols to enhance the site's value in local markets.

To ensure that Corporate America is in compliance with the local legal regulations the manager will make sure that the local legal regulations appear on the global site. The site will comply with foreign trade laws, international sales tax, customs and legality of the content. The laws vary from nation to nation especially when commodities are sold to global customers. For example, France is a country that forbids the sale of any Nazi related items within the demarcation of their nation. The manager want to avoid the tendency to remove the content in the future, thus, after conducting a research on each nation the team in this book will be confident to embed the aforementioned on the web site. The site will sell products to global consumers therefore the foreign trade laws and customers may affect what the company can sell, send, and when the product is sent, how long it will take to get to the destination.

The manager will develop the web site that sponsor various and comprehensive privacy laws. For example, the privacy laws in the European Union are all-embracing than the ones in the United States, in that individuals have freedom to peruse and manage all dossier that any corporation stored about them. In addition, the manager will create the web sites that offer account management tools in order to handle the profiles of customers. The site managers will sponsor tailored services to locales that have different practices from USA domestic markets. For example, the site manager in this book will deliver a personalized service to the satisfactions, desires and tastes of global customers. After conducting online marketing and usability research, the finding will enable the web site managers to personalize global service for the following: (a) local food preferences; (b) customers activities; (c) customers hobby; (d) customers shopping spree; and (e) shopping timeline.

Keeping strings secluded from code so that text can be forwarded to global translation team easily may be the mode of operation for some e-commerce corporations. The corporation in this book will not depend on machine translation. This corporation will hire competent translators. Administering internationalization and localization procedures through a combine approach will be the goal of the corporation. Integrating local terms and concepts specific to each nation on the web sites will be the benchmark of this book. The web sites will show local holidays, currencies, customs, and nonverbal message in the cultures of the global customers. To avoid ambiguity, when depicting date on the web site, the webmaster will entirely spell out the name of the month.

In Corporate America, a corporation might take its operations global by localizing its web site. Some organizations may expand because global markets are more lucrative than domestic markets. To attain economies of scale, organizations may globalize their operations. In order to expand, organizations minimize their dependence on any one market and diversify. Several organizations are expanding their operations globally to accommodate the consumers who are moving abroad. Academic researchers can use the findings of this paper in discussions of identifying target consumers and on how to ensure that the language used on a web site is specific to the country in which it appears. The paper explains how leaders of global corporations determine the need to open warehouses around the world. The manager may have to hire translators. Academic researchers can explore how translators must use languages specific to each nation to write the web contents, products, pop-up advertisements and commercials.

CHAPTER 5
How To Effectively Collaborate

There are seven steps for implementing a collaborative planning, forecasting and replenishment project. The first step is to decide on participating supplies, allowing all parties to know who is involved and who is not. This next step is to agree on the scope of the collaboration, the scope should cover the necessary basics without going beyond the reach of the active parties abilities. After that supporting software should be selected. The selection of supporting software is an important step since without the software the system will not function. The fourth step is to examine the value chain; this step is where the logistics of the system are determined. Next a specific project should be selected. The specific project should match the scope of the collaboration and accomplish the objectives of the system. The sixth step is to develop collaborative solutions. During this step all of the collaborators should communicating to develop solutions for the project and any problems encountered. Finally, the results should be used to make better decisions in the future.

The following are benefits of group work: It provides learning groups are better than individuals at understanding. People readily take ownership of problems and their solutions. They take responsibility. Group members have their egos embedded in the decision, so they are committed to the solution. A group has more information than anyone member. Group members can combine their knowledge to create new knowledge. A group may produce synergy during problem solving. The effectiveness and/or quality of group work can be greater than the sum of what is produced by individuals. Working in a group may simulate creativity of the participants of the process. A group may have better and more precise communication working together.
Risk propensity is balanced. Groups moderate high-risk takers and encourage conservatives.

The four cells frameworks of time and space in communications are: Same time/same place – Participants meet face-to-face in one place at the same time, as in a traditional meeting or decision room. This is still an important way to meet, even when web-based support is used, because it is sometimes critical for participants to leave the office to eliminate distractions. Same time/different place – participants are in different places, but they communicate at the same time. Different time/different place – Participants are in different places, and they also send and receive information at different times. This occurs when team members are traveling, have conflicting schedules or work in different time zones.

The three categories in groupware products as: General - The general category of Groupware products can be either synchronous or asynchronous. It contains features such as peer-to-peer networks, shared screen or built in email. Synchronous – the synchronous category of Groupware products occurs at the same time, examples of this are instant messaging, shared whiteboard, and polling. Asynchronous – the asynchronous category of Groupware products occurs at different times. Some examples of asynchronous Groupware are bulletin boards, blogs and threaded discussions.

The major characteristics of group decision support systems to make business decision are: Its goal is to support the process of group decision makers by providing automation of sub processes, using information technology tools. It is a specially designed information system, not merely a configuration of already existing system components. It encourages generation of ideas, resolution of conflicts, and freedom of expression. It contains built-in mechanisms that discourage development of negative group behaviors, such as destructive conflict, miscommunication and groupthink. The activities supported by group decision support systems are: (1) Collaboration (2) Communication Decision (3) Room Mixed-mode facility and (4) Collocated team facility

The major steps in GDSS as listed in Decision Support and Business Intelligence Systems are: Idea generation –

This exploratory step looks at the problem and attempts to develop creative idea about its important features (or alternate solutions in a problem-solving session.) the ideas can have anything to do with the problem; they can be potential solutions, criteria, or mitigating factors. An electronic brainstorming tool is appropriate; its output is a list of idea. Typical time for this step is 30 to 45 minutes. Idea organization – an idea-organizing tool groups the many ideas generated (possibly hundreds) into a list of key issues. The output of this stage is a list of a few key idea (about one for every 20 original ideas) with supporting details. Typical time for this step is 45 to 90 minutes. Prioritization – at this stage, the key ideas are prioritized. The output is a prioritized list of ideas and details. Typical time for this step is 10 to 20 minutes. Additional idea generation – new ideas are generated based on the prioritization of the key ideas. A brainstorming tool that provides structure, such as a topic commentator tool, is appropriate here. The ideas generated are typically focused on solutions. This stage's output may consist of up to 20 ideas for each of the original key ideas. There are three steps for creating a work environment that supports collaboration. Know what you want – the team members should know what they want such as their definition of success. Determine resource constraints – the constraints include everything that might limit the tools available to the team. Determine what technologies can be used to overcome the constraints as determine in step two.

The benefits of VoIP for business users are many. One benefit is that VoIP allows chief communication officers to explore different deployment options. Another benefit is that it lowers the total cost of ownership as well as operating costs. Also, VoIP reduces the hardware requirements on the server side. VoIP provides better security, with encryption and identity management and streamlines workflows by allowing different business processes to be communication enabled. Finally, VoIP replaces business travel with optimized conferencing tools saving time and money. There are four benefits of VoIP for the user. One is that VoIP eliminates unwanted interruptions and unproductive actions by intelligently filtering communications. Two, VoIP provides access to real-time presence information. Three, VoIP can initiate sessions without the need for previously arranged bridges. Finally, Enables participation in conferencing session quickly with a variety of mobile devices. This book will discuss the implementation and challenges of an automated system for ordering more of an item from a warehouse when it is nearly out of stock at a retail store from a warehouse. The book will also give several scenarios which will be used as examples of how such a system can improve the efficiency of a warehouse or retail location. This book then discusses the next generation of automated logistics systems. With the invention of the internet many new and more powerful technologies have begun a rapid rise. One of these technologies is a system that allows a store to automatically order more of a product that is low on stock with minimal or even no human interaction. Such a system can greatly improve the efficacy of both the warehouse and the retail location which use that warehouse as a supply chain.

When implementing a system which will automatically order more of a product there are several challenges that must be addressed in order to create a secure, but efficient system. The first challenge is making the system secure. Secondly, the retail location and the warehouse must both be able to keep track of what items are located at those locations. Third the retail location must be able to send out a communication detailing what products need to be resupplied. The first challenge is easiest to overcome; a Virtual Private Network (VPN) can handle the orders while keeping the communications secure from outside intrusion. A VPN will also keep false orders from being filed by malicious persons bogging down the system with too many orders or costing the users money as products that are not needed are over stocked. The second challenge is to keep track of the stock. Using Radio-frequency Identification (RFID) or their older cousin barcodes can let the computer system know what products are located where as well as allowing the computer system to track the movements of those products.

Finally, the third major challenge of developing an auto order system is the sending of communications between the retail location and the warehouse automatically. By using the methods to solve the second challenge, a retail location can keep track of what products are located on its shelves and when those products are purchased by consumers, once the computer senses that the stock has dropped below the minimum amount. It then sends an automated message to the warehouse for a resupply of that product. The warehouse can then automatically mark that product for shipment so it can be moved to the loading dock and shipped to the needed location. There are many scenarios in which a system that automatically orders products when they become low stock at a retail location could be put to use. Below are two examples of such scenarios. Scenario one which details a retail supply chain that wants to improve the efficacy of their inventory management system while reducing the number of employees necessary. The second scenario details a retail store chain that wants to reduce overhead without losing efficacy. The third scenario details a company moving beyond a simple automated ordering system and on to the next generation of automated logistics computer systems. The pet food company, Straw and Chow, wants to improve the efficacy of which they handle their client's requests, but cannot afford the number of employees required to make a major difference in efficiency and have turned to Hurricane Consulting for advice on how to improve efficiency without a major increase to overhead. Hurricane Consulting recommends that Straw and Chow have developed a computerized automated ordering system to connect their clients directly to the warehouses. Although the initial costs of such a system may outweigh the costs of hiring more employees in the short term, Hurricane Consulting feels that the benefits of such a system as well as the long term costs will be more beneficial to Straw and Chow.

A pet store retail chain is impressed with their food supplier's new found efficacy and has hired Hurricane Consulting, because they wish to replicate the effect with all of their supply vendors. Hurricane Consulting recommends that the retailer work with its vendors to develop a network of automated order systems which will bring the requested increase to efficacy while allowing for a reduction in overhead by requiring fewer employees. Upon implementing this system the pet store retail chain should find a great increase in efficacy as well as many employees who were previously spending many man hours being tied down in logistics being able to accomplish other tasks instead. The supply vendors should also find similar changes in their structure as well as greater effectiveness when dealing with orders sent by the pet store retail chain. Due to the effective at reducing costs and increasing efficiency as implemented in scenario one, Straw and Chow has managed to acquire enough capital to purchase the entire supply chain from the retail store to the factory that produces the food. They have hired Hurricane Consulting to help develop a system to increase the effectiveness and reduce overhead of their new purchase. Hurricane Consulting recommends that Straw and Chow take the next step beyond the automated order system and begin development of a system which will predict supply and demand allowing Strawn and Chow to plan in advance for surges and reductions in demand for their product. While such a system presents many new challenges it is the next logical step in automated logistics and if implemented properly could become extremely profitable for Straw and Chow. In the first two scenarios the automatic ordering system was useful to varying degrees. In the first scenario it did meet the required goal of increasing efficacy without greatly increasing and possibly even reducing, annual costs. However, it is the second scenario where the automatic ordering system truly begins to show its worth. By working with the suppliers the pet store retail chain in able to not only reduce its own overhead while increasing efficacy, but also that of its suppliers as well. These supplies will then most likely choose to pass some of those saving onto the retail chain by reducing the prices for their services. Also, because of the reduced costs to the suppliers they may be able to underbid other suppliers for new contracts allowing them to expand their businesses exponentially and increase their profit margins.

In scenario three Straw and Chow has moved beyond needing just a simple automated order system and has now become the supplier and producer of a product. By taking the next logical step in the evolution of the system discussed in this paper Straw and Chow will move to being on the cutting edge of business intelligence system design and implementation, which should show huge leaps in efficacy and production. As the scenarios demonstrate the automated ordering system is clearly worth the costs of development and use. It is most effective when used on a large scale to connect multiple stores and multiple distribution services, but can be useful on a smaller scale as well. The scenarios clearly demonstrate that the larger the system is the more beneficial the system becomes. A company should not be content to develop only an automatic ordering system but should be constantly looking for new improvements and developments to increase the efficacy of which not only orders are placed, but also the efficacy with which products are developed, manufactured and deployed.

Not everyone can work together and when people work it is necessary to collaborate. Collaboration can be in groups within an organization or with other organizations. In order to collaborate one can manage to utilize several different types of tools to support decision support systems. One of which is through Groupware, Think Tank or with other technology such as GDSS or GSS. All of which utilize the four-cell framework to improve their decision-making skills. All of which allows many people to work together even though they are not in the same location, shift or time zone. When we work in groups and teams it is crucial to maximize creativity, communication, information and our decision-making skills to solve our problems. Organizations can use groupware, Internet, intranet, extranet and many other collaboration tools to improve decision-making that will affect an organization.

There are benefits of working in groups according to Technology Insights: It provides learning. Groups are better than individuals at understanding problems. People readily take ownership of problems and their solutions. They take responsibility. Group members have their egos embedded in the decision, and so they are committed to the solution. Groups are better than individuals at catching errors. A group has more information (i.e., knowledge) than any one member. Group members can combine this knowledge to create new knowledge. More and more creative alternatives for problem solving can be generated, and better solutions can be derived (e.g., through stimulation). A group may produce synergy during problem solving. The effectiveness and/or quality of group work can be greater than the sum of what is produced by independent individuals. Working in a group may stimulate the creativity of the participants and the process. A group may have better and more precise communication working together. Risk propensity is balanced. Groups moderate high-risk takers and encourage conservatives.

Groupware will support decision making directly and indirectly such as the four cell technology allows the following scenarios: (1) Same time/same place. Participants meet face-to-face in one place at the same time, as in a traditional meeting or decision room. This is still an important way to meet, even when Web-based support is used, because it is sometimes critical for participants to leave the office to eliminate distractions. (2) Same time/different place. Participants are in different places, but they communicate at the same time, for example, with videoconferencing. (3) Different time/same place. People work in shifts. One shift leaves information for the next shift. (4) Different time/different place (any time, any place). Participants are in different places. They also send and receive information at different times. This occurs when team members are traveling, have conflicting schedules, or work in different time zones.

The three categories of groupware products are as follows:

General Synchronous and Asynchronous

(1)Built-in e-mail and messaging system. (2) Browser interface. (3) Joint Web-page creation. (4) Sharing of active hyperlinks. (5) File sharing (graphics, video, audio, or other). (6) Built-in search functions (by topic or keyword). (7) Workflow tools. (8) Use of corporate portals for communication, (9) collaboration, and search. (10) Shared screens. (11) Electronic decision rooms. (12) Peer-to-peer networks.

Synchronous (same-time)

(1)Instant messaging (IM). (2) Videoconferencing and multimedia conferencing. (3) Audio conferencing. (4) Shared whiteboard and smart whiteboard. (5) Instant video. (6) Brainstorming. (7) Polling (voting), and (8) other decision support (consensus builder, scheduler).

Asynchronous (different times)

(1)Workspaces. (2) Threaded discussions. (3) Users can receive and send e-mail, SMS. (4) Users can receive activity notification alerts, (5) via e-mail or SMS. (6) Users can/expand discussion threads. (7) Users can sort messages (by date, author, or read/unread). (8) Auto responder. (9) Chat session logs. (10) Bulletin boards and discussion groups. (11) Use of blogs, (12) wikis, and wikilogs. (13) Collaborative planning and/or design tools. (14) Use of bulletin boards.

There are three major characteristics of Group Decision Support Systems according to: Its goal is to support the process of group decision makers by providing automation of sub processes using information technology tools. It is a specially designed information system, not merely a configuration of already-existing system components. It can be designed to address one type of problem or a variety of group-level organizational decisions. It encourages generation of ideas, resolution of conflicts, and freedom of expression. It contains built-in mechanisms that discourage development of negative group behaviors such as destructive conflict miscommunication and groupthink.

In order to support and improve productivity and effectiveness of meetings one can follow the following activities: (1) Supports parallel processing of information and idea generation (parallelism). (2) Enables the participation of larger groups with more complete information, knowledge, and skills. (3) Permits the group to use structured or unstructured techniques and methods. (4) Offers rapid, easy access to external information. Allows parallel computer discussions. (5) Helps participants frame the big picture. (6) Anonymity allows shy people to contribute to the meeting (get up and do what needs to be done). (7) Anonymity helps prevent aggressive individuals from driving the meeting. Provides for multiple ways to participate in instant, anonymous voting. (8) Provides structure for the planning process to keep the group on track. Enables several users to interact simultaneously (conferencing). (9) Records all information presented at the meeting (organizational memory).

When making decisions there are four major steps to follow: (1) Idea generation: This exploratory step looks at the problem and attempts to develop creative ideas about its important features. (2) Idea organization: An idea-organizing tool groups the many ideas generated into a list of key issues. (3) The output of this stage is a list of a few key ideas with the supporting details. (4) Prioritization: At this stage, the key ideas are prioritized. (5) A voting tool can be appropriate. (6) Additional idea generation: New ideas are generated based on the prioritization of the key ideas. (7) A brainstorming tool that provides structure, such as a topic commentator, is appropriate here.

In order to motivate employees the managers should know the following steps: Know what you want: Get team members to articulate their definition of success (or performance). This is part of the team-building process. Determine resource constraints: These include everything from the geographic distribution of team members to reporting relationships to motivations. Each constraint limits the possible tools the team can use. Determine what technologies can be used to overcome resource constraints: It is important to keep in mind business needs rather than fun, new, or convenient technologies.

VoIP communication is the internet's telephone system which helps company's keep cost down while boosting efficiency: Allows CIOs to explore different deployment options for company's communications needs. Lowers total cost of ownership (TCO) through voice/data convergence. Lowers operational costs through use of integrated applications. Reduces hardware requirements on the server side for certain applications. Provides a holistic approach to security, enhanced by encryption and identity management. Helps streamline workflows by empowering companies to communications-enable different business processes. Enables optimized conferencing tools to replace business travel.

VoIP benefits not only business but also the individual at home or at work: (1) eliminates unwanted interruptions and unproductive actions by intelligently filtering communications. (2) Provides access to real-time presence information, which helps decisions get made faster. (3) Initiates ad-hoc conferencing/collaboration sessions without the need to pre-arranging separate audio- or videoconferencing bridges. (4) Enables participation in conferencing sessions quickly and easily via a variety of mobile devices. (5) Before implementing a CPFR project one should follow the seven steps: Decide on participating suppliers. (6) Agree on the scope of collaboration. (7) Select support software. (8) Examine the value chain. (9) Determine a specific project. (10) Develop collaborative solutions. (11) Use the results for better decisions.

When we work in groups and teams it is crucial to maximize creativity, communication, information and our decision-making skills to solve our problems. Teamwork is crucial to any organization in today's market to solve their complex problems. When we work it takes more than one person to come up with the best possible solution. By establishing relationships one can manage to utilize several different types of tools to support decision support systems. There are some well-known tools like Groupware, Think Tank and other technology such as GDSS or GSS. By utilizing the four-cell framework to improve decision-making skills it allows more people to work together even though they are not in the same location, shift or time zone. Organizations can use groupware, Internet, intranet, extranet and many other collaboration tools to improve decision-making that will affect an organization.

One should be proud to announce that Internet banking is a success in every measure. The online banking is so lucrative to the extent that Intuit Inc., the parent of QuickBooks, decided to procure the Digital Insight Inc., for the total amount of cash along with debt of $1.35 billion. At the same time, the benefits attributable to this combination are the following: sound financial management, tax software, the ingenuity of QuickBooks, online banking services, timely delivery systems, and vast number of e-banking customers. The purpose of this paper is to elucidate about how online banking industries supports sound operational practices, configuration, and management practices. Furthermore, this paper will help ascertain if merchant bankers are in compliance with empirical business protocol. In addition, this paper will establish if the available resources and technology tools are being utilized as effectively and efficiently as possible. The body of the paper will discuss the concepts behind Internet banking logistics, remunerations; article of trade; distribution; pricing strategies; promotional campaign, online security compliance, price and endowment; conditions, findings and recommendations. Let us now look into the logistics of the Internet banking.

The Netbank is the first company located in the United States that eventually inaugurated online banking and in 1996, the Wingspan Company emulated Netbank. However, the extant traditional banks were essentially innovative in developing the initial telephone banking system but were wrongly hesitant to use online technology prior to 1998. Surprisingly, in 2000, the well-known National bank accrued overwhelming market share because this organization went online when throngs of customers became online banking enthusiasts. Whereas, one finds that about 13 million people perform the following daily online banking transactions, namely, imputing checking, loan, credit card account and paying bill online.

The population of the households that now participates in online banking amount to 40 million; and this is one third of all U.S. household members. Similarly, the numbers will continue to grow; possibly reaching 52 million household members that will bank online. On the other hand, several online banks possess the courtesy of permitting their customers to migrate their money online for free. For instance, the following amenities are seen on the online banking bill payment: (1) To your payees; (2) express payments, (3) make one-time payment, (4) set up a recurring payment, (5) future payments (see, change, or cancel), (6) payment history (including open payments), (7) cancelled payments, (8) add a new payee, see, change or delete payees, (9) payee spending report, (10) report a bill payment problem, and (11) make a transfer payment.

Globally, several organizations are constantly busy innovating technologically driven processes to make banking services convenient and available on consumer cell phones. For instance, a company by the name of Firethorn Holdings LLC allocates the company software for phone installation. Another candidate, Clairmail Inc., seized the advantages of text messages protocol, which are abundantly available on several customers cell phone. Similarly, online-banking software of Corillian Corp is now currently operating on cell phone browser. Society is now aware that the infamous online resources of Corillian Corp now inaugurate the mobile phone banking product. In addition, let us talk about the major achievement of the Chantilly payment technology vendor who has recently migrated data from online banks Web sites on to mobile cell phone. We know that the strategy in trend is to use software to generate revenue and differentiate to business segments from the competitors.

The continuous expansion of profits in online savings accounts has enabled consumers to enjoy ebanking as it usually pays higher yields. Meanwhile, the difference is clear, online banking is not like the extant traditional banks because enrolled customers are treated with paperless statements. They enjoy paying bills online; and make deposits electronically or by traditional snow mail. Another convenient feature is that online customers can withdraw their dollars from drive-through ATM networks. For instance, the prominent Citibank, though an offline bank, has constructed its high yield online savings accounts to prevent massive customer withdrawal of money from their accounts. The net assets of Citibank online saving account have reached geometric proportions of $112.5 billion. The next paragraph discusses remunerations, also known as recompense of great reward.

This study observes two core abilities, on one hand is the propensity to financially induce the potential customers and on the other hand is the trend to give monetary incentive to the employees. For instance, there is availability of customers rebate, quality certificate and pay back guarantee that management may use to switch potential customers. The banking industries should be cognizance that employees, at times, perform above and beyond the call of duty and/or consistently maintain a level of performance that distinguishes them from their co-workers. Thus, customer switch incentive program should be designed to recognize and reward employees who have rendered services consistently above average or at an excellent level. The banking industries should place a high value on professional, courteous, caring, customer switching productivity and helpful services to the consumers. Conversely, employees who receive in excess of two confirmed complaints in a quarter should not qualify for customer switch incentive reward during that quarter. Performance incentive is critical element that will ensure organizational goal achievement, productivity and positive result.

The latent customers of online banks are still waiting to be persuaded to become believer, converts and adopt banking online. Thus, blame it on the responsibilities of the merchant bankers who are not diligent enough to persuade the potential consumers. Conversely, one may want to know the debilitating effects of the following factors: (1) as notorious as it is, 35% out of the total segment of banks have online links, furthermore, the web pages are deficient in description of the benefit and advantages of ebanking. (2) Very funny, only one-third of the banking industry engages customers on the operations and services tutorial. (3)

Surprisingly, only 35% of the bankers elucidate about the rewards achievable by becoming online banking converts. (4) In 2003, banks still repeated their previous mode of inactive operations. The information on the Web site still remains legacy, intact and had never been altered.

The bill payment is a main priority of several consumers; however, this bothered several schools of thought as to why it was not being glorified on the Web sites. Furthermore, one finds that the bankers were reluctant to explain the bill payment and other services as early as possible to the customers and possible candidates. Given that the bill payment is indispensable to all society, however, the timeliness and reward derivable from online banking innovations were not adequately emphasized to the populace (Sarel and Marmorstein, 2004, March). Accordingly, the Edge Company successfully crafted ACH-based system and now customers pay their bill to the stockbroker from online bank account, pay dentist, buy ebay auction, and transfer money from coast to coast in the United States, even globally. All credit and power to San Jeev Dheer who pioneered Cash Edge simplifying inter-bank monetary transfer. The ACH system of migrating e-money has made banking industry to achieve the payment technological attainment, further minimizing the business transactional cost. Let us now peruse the price and endowment.

This is a known fact that merchant bankers permit both of the online banking converts and non-converts absolutely free access to their Web sites. Given that several bankers offer bill payment and other services in their individual segment, outstanding dissimilarity, though, were found in the price tag charged for bill payment services. However, fees were taken from the consumer for using bill payment and other services this was common in the period before 2002. Thus, incentives were not provided to the customers who had abundant fund, loan and investment with online bankers. Instead of using bill payment capabilities as an incentive to attract and retain customers the merchant banker did not recognize the market power they had in their arsenal. The year 2003 brought about the percentage increase in inducement of customer with the consideration of free bill payment to all. Nevertheless, 60% percentages of the online bankers are still adamant in collecting fee for bill payment service.

Consequently, the best mode of operation is to empower the management that occupy the higher echelon of organization to handle conversion of customers by influencing the productivity of their employees or customer services through incentives for individual and/or team achievement. Several organizations normally implement an incentive pay program that recognizes employee efficiency and performance by rewarding contributions to each organization goals and objectives. Meanwhile, organization should establish a mechanism of punishment for deficient or deteriorating performance and provide incentive for future performance and improved productivity. The society is now aware of many recognition programs to acknowledge employee contributions, usually non-cash such as employee awards, recognition, celebration and gifts for a job well done. This can be provided for individual and for teams.

Scholarly community is aware that financial and any incentive encourages customers to adopt a product thereby become an organizational convert. Conversely, the finding is obvious that several bankers refused to use any inducement to stimulate customers to adopt new actions and switch to online banking. Meanwhile, there was a minor progression in 2003 because 4.8 per cent bankers gave non-financial reward to customer that use bill payment. However, in advocating for customers to use bill payment service, 95.2 per cent bankers are against using financial stimulus.

In the same token, the management should work with their workforce to put the incentive plan into implementation. They must establish eligibility criteria for market and performance adjustments. Executive staff's objectives in this area are to establish criteria that focus on high performance with at least three months of customer history with the bankers. Online banking has historically experienced high turnover and/or difficulties in obtaining prospective customers.

Incentive atmosphere should have been developed to improve competitiveness in the online market and reduce consumer turnover. Obtaining and retaining customers represent top priorities for market adjustments. Executive staff should recommend strong emphasis on staff performance and thereby device an employee performance incentive. Banker employees must earn performance awards each year, independent from prior year performance or awards. This should provide a powerful incentive tool for continued strong services delivery and financial performance. The following paragraph will allow one to peruse article of trade.

In view of the fact that online banking bill payment process is indispensable thus organization should not make it a secluded alternative but as a primary component of the total online banking services. Correspondingly, all online benefits, namely, fund transfer or email alert should be components of the online banking package. Meanwhile, one needs to simplify online registration process for the benefit of new online converts. Similarly, organization needs to grant consumers less fatigue activities hence they will yearn to switch to online banking. Organizational effectiveness promotes values when adapting to change, other ways to accomplish effectiveness includes implementing online banking process improvement, projecting cost and efficiency savings, ensuring continuous improvement, quality control and providing staff cross training and development. The next paragraph will allow us to peruse the system of circulation.

If several organization is doing it, online banks should not be an exception to the rule therefore management should use several channels to proffer the online bank services. Similarly, online banking exhibition material, presentation and matriculation must be accessible to all stakeholders. The consumers should see where to activate, initiate or conclude an online banking service in a multiple geographical locations thus bankers should make it available on the Web sites; offline; mall, marketplaces, offices, Schools, legacy branch; and on the cell phone. Conversely, given the precedent set by several prominent merchant bankers, it is inconceivable for potential customers to visit a local office in order to conclude the initiation of an online bank account. Let us now peruse the payment strategies.

Online merchant banker should discourage upholding their online services as a self-governing profit center. In addition, banker should proffer inexpensive pricing to entice latent customers to the online banking. For example, customers experience free bank account and all online banking experience with Washington Mutual bank. A bad idea is to encourage merchant bankers to put price tag on bill payment and other services because implementing that ill-conceived decision will prevent customers from conversion. However, merchant banker should know how to craft strategic design that is all-inclusive to attract target customer to sign new account and maintain a lucrative relationship. Similarly, one would encourage merchant banker to use package of services at one price to benefit customers. Nevertheless, an overzealous pricing policy will eventually discourage customers and disallow them to adopt online channel. Consequently, online banker can procure their revenue or profit on global scale through investing or conducting overnight selling of money. One can now peruse the promotional campaign in the next paragraph.

Meanwhile, an astute observer now finds that, three to four percent of online participants, this is equivalent to 63 million American adults that performed their individual banking transactions via online in December 2005. However, the research community did not notice any substantive progress in 2004. Consequently, the Pew Internet & American Life Project (PIALP) eventually confirmed that flat increases of consumers banking online ensued. This is contrary to the overall maximization of Internet users; PIALP therefore concluded that the society might be suffering from lack of confidence on online banking.

One may positively surmise that the feasible solution to flat increases may be the advent of promotional campaign. The best way for an online organization to utilize its operations to change the future performance is to embark on customer care that is based on providing quality customer service on a daily basis (Orr, 2004, May). One thing is clear, the online banking encourages: (1) satisfaction, (2) organizations competitiveness, (3) innovation (4) creativity (5) cheaper cost, (6) convenient (7) modernizes financial products, and (8) lower investment in traditional bank. In a nutshell, one knows that it would be more expedient, and profitable for online organizations to inculcate these benefits into the thought processes of their employees and potential customers.

Online banking does not routinely require the employees to use promotional items to solicit customer conversion on the Internet. Assertively, organization should try all electronic technology and high pace digital media to disseminate their special incentives programs inviting probable consumer to attempt the service. The promotional campaign should use notice board in offline branch to carry announcements, banner ads, posters and flyers. In addition, merchant banker can use e-mail promotions, direct mail, junk mail, and statement inserts. The employees should be given incentive to invite friends and neighbors to sign up. Telephone representatives have the capabilities to enlist a successful convert. In either case, company should distribute a recompense of great reward to employees that successfully and consistently convert customers.

Objectively, management responsibility is to persuade employees to ask consumer to tryout, exhibit usage and facilitate online banking enlistment. Otherwise, the success stories of the banks in Finland should be adopted in the USA. For instance, in Finland potential consumers are normally invited to receive free practical tutorial at the offices of the merchant bankers. Consequently, online merchant bankers should be knowledgeable about the precise worry of diverse segments and use inducement to get people to act now. A good recommendation would be to provide the proper guidance to carry out promotional strategy via all media channel. The management of the online organization should detail comprehensive workforce responsibilities to provide adequate guidance for the control and efficient operation.

The bank industry should embark on sales promotion

by beguiling imminent customers to immediately encounter online banking and bill payment. In order to be able to induce prospects to encounter online baking, management must provide pragmatic experiment, incentive, rebate and options that are conducive to various segments. A standing example is Bank of America that has instituted in branch experimentation of online banking and reports about the positive customers enjoyment and revenue enlargement. Meanwhile, the sales promotion method has been quite successful for those banks that provide financial incentives. Consequently, bankers are hereby encouraged to use monetary inducement to cleverly ask prospective customers to open account and continuous usage of online banking services. Moreover, one should bait customers in order to enhance new habitual characteristics thus online bankers should encourage them to incessantly use bill payment and other services. For example, Citibank invented and implemented financial incentives to stimulate customers to encounter hence get addicted to online banking services.

Furthermore, merchant bankers should craft different aspect of state of the art promotional tools on the online menu contents and acceptance procedures. Consequently, one should enlighten merchant bankers to alter their strategic thought process of products administration in exchange for customer relationship management. Customer driven motivations and satisfactions should be sole focus of online banking business, which is based on providing quality customer service on a daily basis to both internal and external customers. Organization should grant customers rebate, quality certificate and pay back guarantee in order to build trust, loyalty and customer retention. In order to cover all households, like American Online, online banking industry should mail out free audio and video tutorial program that also contains monetary incentive for successful customer referrer. The next paragraph will allow one to see the online security compliance.

Merchant bankers have wrong assumption that the customers are merely persuaded simply by the announcement of online banking services; this is absolutely a wrong thinking that latent consumers are desperate for the online banking sophistication and innovation. In the same token, several organization marketing strategies focuses only on telling the consumer about the availability of the product is enough to warrant the interest of the consumer. For instance, the webs sites were constructed to be operational with little endeavor to communicate real benefits to consumers. In most cases the initial online experience did very little to influence or inspire customers to try the service. Pricing did not assist either. Charges for bill payment are infamous, as banks comply with their traditional cost-plus approach to pricing.

The availability of live customer services to assist customers and the opportunity to aid them in the enrollment process is not entertained. Surprisingly, some organization normally protects or even conceals the telephone numbers of customer service representative. Nevertheless, there are vestiges of banks (for instance Citibank) have been more assertive in promoting intensive marketing standards, however, the entire industry are wrongly convinced that the society does not need any live customer service call center or persuasions, that customers are yearning to embark on online banking. Meanwhile, some revolutionary banks have taken the leap of leadership and are practicing successful strategies of customer cares, call center, live customer services and persuasions; however, the mainstream of the industry retained the common protocol.

In addition, the majority of the new merchant bankers are following traditional strategies. In sum total, their approach depicts lack of business knowledge of the outstanding issues. The new merchant bankers are yet to decipher the best approach to induce and hasten consumer to enlist in online banking. Conversely, the poignant issues are that the consumer may not comprehend the matchlessness of online process, they don't want to temper with it, and they don't like the price tag, security risk and fraud. Thus, merchant bankers had better device brand new strategies. When the potential customers are not adequately persuaded, consequently, they refuse to become a consumer.

To normalize this anomaly management should advance marketing strategies to this group of nonchalant consumer. This strategy can be easily implemented without significant strain on management.

The consumer study depicted many deplorable impediments to speedy switch to online banking, by and large; there is a little growth in the numbers of online banking consumers. However, the customers who are actively involved appreciate the online service. Consequently, the advantages derivable ranges from comfort, timesaving, empowerment and combination of financial services were highly glamorous. In addition, consumers are easily acclimated once becoming active participant thereafter the clarity of the benefits is assimilated. Meanwhile, the bill payment capabilities are the valuable favorite of the satisfied customers. Though customers were first attracted by common enthusiasm of the online services of bill payment accessibilities and eventually became ardent believers in the doctrine of the online banking systems. The public that is not yet interested in Internet should be cordially invited to banking ground locations where the bankers give them free training.

One can now confidently prognosticate that the imminent customers are bound to equally prefer the benefit of online bill payment. Another thing is certain, encounter, trial and continuous usage of online banking amenities will obviously convince people. Then, merchant bankers should accurately deduce the strategy and bait to favorably induce the forthcoming customers. In order to woo potential customers to acknowledge the inherent conveniences and rewards available in online banking the management may have to consider two diverse methods. These diverse methods are popularly known as traditional communication learning or experiential learning methods.

Research finding postulated that the market is always available for un-haunted innovation, therefore, experiential learning method is highly recommended. The good news is that banks are now tackling the case of nonchalant consumer. Meanwhile, the bank industries should not be advised to use the slow process of communication learning methods because it is inefficient and inadequate to convince imminent customers. For that reason assertive methods should be utilized to induce consumer encounter with online bank services. Accordingly, progressive banks are cost efficient. The vast spending on traditional advertisement should be eliminated. One prominent example is the Bank of American. Thus, online bankers should focus on advancing promotions via experiential learning method.

In 2003, several bankers were advocating about online aspect of security, one thing common and noticeable is the lip service perpetrated by the bankers therefore; the potential customers remain alert to be persuaded. Interestingly, in the year 2006, the bank regulators of United States promulgated passmark's multifactor authentication security requirement. Consequently, the following are the current steps taken by a few members of e-bank industries in order to comply with the online security process: (1) Fauquier bank anticipate to comply with multifactor authentication by having consumers provide their picture, phrase and/or customers personal computer will be registered according to individual location thus the picture and phrase will become the default process. (2) Fauquier says that multifactor authentication for business Internet banking will be in full swing in the month of February 2007, while the Internet banking for customers will be effective in the month of April 2007. Fauquier says that on January 1, 2007 is the time period when general email will be posted to inform consumers to be ready for the update in secure bank e-mail and the banker also anticipate using secure bank email process to inform all the customers in order to minimize the cost of dissemination.

In the same token, (1) MC Bank is now in compliance with multifactor authentication by combining the gadget to Internet banking products. This strong security system works in unison with online banking browser application. (2) MC Bank demonstrated that multifactor authentication for business Internet banking was effective in the month of December 2006. (3) MC Bank gave the customer a brochure with passmark security operating manual including a letter about the levels of security. The regulator strongly recommends online banking security performance. Thus, the bank industry should submit it security program criteria recommendation for the review and approval of the regulators. Security reassurance information should be widely publicized to all people through all channels.

    This book has articulated how Internet banking is a success in every measure. The purposes of this research paper has been served in the realms of how banking industries supports the concepts of Internet banking logistics, benefits, remunerations; price and endowment; article of trade; distribution; pricing strategies; and promotional campaign, online security compliance, Conditions, findings and recommendations. Meanwhile, Internet has developed new lucrative areas of online banking. Accordingly, the security innovations are noted in the body of this book because organization management has recently implemented procedures to ensure that all the security promulgations are complied with.

CHAPTER 6
The Home Depot Inc.

According to a study by Stanford University, one-third of all U.S. consumers believe global warming is the most serious ecological issue facing the world today. More than half the respondents view this issue as extremely or very important; almost double the number just a decade ago. The paper will explore how The Home Depot responded to consumer's demands for more green products. The Home Depot implemented the economic and ecological options that boosted the profit margins of the organization. The most important external forces impinging on the Ford Motor Company and The Home Depot are both Economic and Ecological. Since the economic factors in the external environment are largely macroeconomic, there are two microeconomic factors that Home Depot should be concerned with: They are Growth rates, and Levels of employment. For Home Depot, the levels of employment could have a negative effect on customer's ability to invest in home improvement needs. They might purchase more basic necessities, but they won't be interested in large purchases that tend to incur more personal debt.

The same could be said of the growth rate of a business expanding or contracting due to recession. The next area of concern from external forces would be the Ecological factors. Home Depot is in the business of selling all kinds of products that tend to have a negative effect on the natural environment. They will have to respond to consumer demand for more environmentally friendly products in they intend to maintain a strategic advantage. The business managers can no longer segregate the natural and the business world; they are inseparably linked. The Ford Motor Company has a few important external forces impinging upon their bottom line as well.

In response to demand Home Depot launched

a new product label in 2007 called Eco Options. Eco
Options uses strict ecologically friendly criteria to
designate their products under this label. The desire
to earn the Eco Options label spurred Home Depot's
suppliers to produce even more eco-friendly products.
Not to be out done by Home Depot, their competitor
Lowe's, soon began to introduce organic gardening
supplies, fertilizer, soil, and insecticides. By applying a
PESTEL analysis to both Home Depot and Ford
Motor Company they are able to determine the most
important external forces affecting each company.
The PESTEL analysis includes an examination of the
political, economic, socio-cultural, technological,
ecological, and legal forces that may or may not
impact the performance of a company. The political
environment describes the processes and actions of
government bodies that influence the decisions and
behavior of firms. Home Depot is considered an
oligopoly where there are few sellers in the industry.
One of the key features of an oligopoly is that
competing firms are interdependent and non-price
competition is the preferred mode of competition. Of
course Home Depot must be aware that price fixing is
illegal.

The ecological factors has to do with the increased
customer desire and awareness of air pollution and cars with
engines that produce less carbon emissions and deliver more
power. Should the pressure from consumers increase in the
near future, the Ford Motor Company will certainly come
under pressure to compete for market share to gain strategic
advantage. Finally, there is also the economic forces that will
impinge upon the company should interest rates and levels
of employment become an issue. In should go without saying
that during times of high unemployment and economic
slowdown, people will not be interested in making such a
large investment no matter how low the interest rates are.
The ethical decision making can sometime follow the maxim:
in the eye of the beholder. There are those that say that there
is no such thing as business ethics. It is often referred to as

an oxymoron-a concept that combines opposite or contradictory ideas. There is no worldwide standard for business people. Sometimes companies will engage in unethical behavior without realizing it. Business people can disagree about what is considered ethical due to differences in value perceptions. There are some business people who legitimately believe that profit maximization is the key goal of their firm, whereas concerned interest groups may have other priorities.

Ethics is defined as the consensually accepted standards of behavior for an occupation, trade, or profession. The problem here is that the difference in values can make it difficult for one group to understand another's actions. In a free market system the term "let the buyer beware" is a traditional comment. The argument here is that customers have the right to choose how they spend their money and live their lives. Likewise, a business has the right to maximize profits if it is for the greater good of the company and doesn't adversely disadvantage consumers. In the view of this writer, it is unethical to deceive, undermine, lie, or disadvantage another person for one's own selfish purposes. The mislabeling of products fits this description.

Companies can turn threats into opportunities by putting in place the kind of activities that will allow the firm to dynamically respond to changing consumer demand. A careful SWOT analysis of the Home Depot would conclude that the company could suffer the most from an ecological awareness by its customers due to the type of products that they sell that impact the environment. However, it is clear that the Home Depot's efforts to respond with their Eco Options brand is a sure sign that this company has taken the necessary steps to turn an external ecological threat into an opportunity. When I apply the VRIO framework to assess the company's internal competitive advantage I see that the introduction the Eco Options program provides the firm with a resource that is Valuable, Rare, costly for others to Imitate, and they appear to be Organized to capture and fully exploit the resources value. As for the Ford Motor Company, they too have before them an external threat that must be taken into account from an ecological and economic standpoint.

The focus here would be the threat of not responding to the customer's desire for more eco-friendly hybrid-type vehicles with comparably powered engines. However, according to the Ford Motor Company website, this company has already turned a potential external threat into an opportunity for sustained competitive advantage. Their website touts outlines the company's efforts to prevent or reduce the potential for environmental, economic and social harm due to climate change. The site goes on to discuss their science-based strategy to reduce greenhouse gas emissions from their products, with an increased focus on doing their part to stabilize carbon dioxide concentrations in the atmosphere. There is also a section that discussed their efforts to continue greening their products moving forward.

From the standpoint of economic value created I can assume that Home Depot's Eco Options is a positive contributor. There is over 4,000 stock-keeping units that carry the Eco Options label brought in about $2.2 billion in sales and the brand is growing fast. Although accounting data may capture some intangible assets, many key intangible assets are not captured. Indeed, intangibles that are not captured in accounting data such as a firm's reputation for quality and innovation or superior customer service have become much more important in firm stock market valuations over the last few decades. For Home Depot, the accounting profitability can be best measured by the intangible assets that they possess. As for shareholder value, the average customer's purchase basket that contains an Eco Options product was $107, compared with an overall average of $58; implying that the Eco Options label garnered an 85 percent price premium. In light of these numbers, if the trend continues the total return to shareholders, which is the return on risk capital, including stock price appreciation plus dividends received over a specific period, should provide a measurable dividend.

When it comes to the balanced scorecard approach, The Home Depot will certainly benefit from this type of managerial practice because it will allow managers to communicate and link the Eco Options strategy to all responsible parties with the organization. They will next have the ability to translate this vision into measureable operational goals. The Eco Options give the company the basis to design and plan processes; and finally, through Eco Options, management will more easily implement feedback and organizational learning in order to modify and adapt strategic goals when indicated.

When it comes to the triple bottom line which is the combination of economic, social, and ecological concerns that can lead to a sustainable strategy, The Home Depot is certainly on the front lines in this case. The Eco Options labeling program puts this company on the forefront when it comes to focusing on the social, ecological, and economic concerns of its customers, strategic stakeholder, and partners.

The Home Depot has stood up to the challenge of addressing the consumer demands for a diverse range of products that are ecologically made with the maintenance of the environment in mind. As a result, the company launched its eco-options line that specifically targeted those products in response; thus, transforming and external treat into an opportunity for profitability. The Ford Motor Company's implementation of manufacturing electric vehicles is another example of how a company is able to maintain its competitive advantage by creating goals and objectives that addresses external threats by utilizing the company's internal strengths in order to generate opportunity. The external forces impinging upon the Home Depot and the Ford Motor Co. are different as the Home Depot has been imposed by ecological and socio-cultural attributes and the Ford Motor Co. is affected by external forces that are political with a combination of technological and economical attributes. As Home Depot responded to consumer's demands for more green products, in response, Home Depot launched a new product label called Eco Options that designated products within its supple as ecologically friendly. With Home Depot's suppliers wanting to be included in this specialized line of products, interested suppliers developed more innovative ways to incorporate its products. The eco options brand makes it easy for consumers to identify products that make a difference, one choice at a time. Every product with the eco-options label has less of an impact on the environment than competing products. Specifically, eco - options products offer one or more of the following benefits: Energy Efficiency, Water Conservation, Healthy Home, Clean Air, and Sustainable Forestry. (2) These items included super low-flow toilets and energy efficient appliances and lighting, thus Home Depot initiating the ecological phenomenon in home improvement.

Home Depot was affected by the socio-cultural affects externally due to consumer demands for Eco friendly products. With these consumers having a culture that is sensitive to the affects that products may have on the environment, Home Depot incorporated these concerns in its marketing plan by developing and launching the Eco Options product label. As the community of consumers, for which the Home Depot services, lives a lifestyle congruent with values that are concerned with environmental awareness, developing such line as Eco Options demonstrates Home Depot's response to its external socio-culture atmosphere. With regards to the Ford Motor Co., the political and economic external affects were most impinging. As Ford, GM, and Chrysler maintained a monopoly in the automobile industry for most of the 20th century, the foreign entrants strengthened competition while threatening Ford's market shares. (1) To address the political effects on development once imposed, these foreign entities built U.S. plants in order to evade import restrictions. Ford was also affected economically due to the expense of the production of its product as the company needed to manufacture its fleet on a larger scale. As a result of this imposition of cost, Ford began to generate its own electric vehicles. Innovating electrification technologies is a key element of Ford's broader approach of manufacturing vehicles that have improved fuel economy and reduced greenhouse emissions. (3) Do to a consumer demand for more technological innovations;

electric vehicles have become more prevalent.

It is undetermined at this time whether or not the Home Depot has caught the "Green Wave" or is "Green washing". If the company fails to expand within the community in order to assist with the overall transition to a more environment conscious lifestyle for all citizens, it could be believed that it is simply capitalizing on the consumer's demand for more Ego friendly products, thus generating income. Merely establishing a line of products that target the need to address the preservation of the environment isn't a demonstration of a true depiction of a company's value towards the issue. Marty Neumeier, founder and president of Neutron, a San Francisco-based firm specializing in brand partnership, also offered caveat that the most effective eco-label can't fix a larger branding or marketing problem. He cites Home Depot as an example. It is not ethical to charge an increased price for the Eco friendly products if these products do not warrant this increase due to an increase in expense to acquire from the manufacturer. However, if the increase in price included an established amount to be donated to the cause for improving the environment, and such donation was equal to the difference between the original and escalated price, then such increase is warranted. Creating an elevated price for these specialized products would suggest that the consumers who are expected to purchase these items are targeted and discriminated against because of its preference.

The SWOT analysis could be used to determine which of the two companies, the Home Depot or the Ford Motor Co., has a stronger ecological awareness by consumers as a threat and as an opportunity. It appears that the Home Depot is threatened more by the ecological awareness of consumers as it attempts to sell products that have the potential to damage the environment. However, it appears that the company has turned the threat into an opportunity by developing the Eco Options line of earth friendly products. The Ford Motor Company is less threatened by this same consumer awareness, as consumers are less demanding of vehicles that maintain environmental quality than their demand for home improvement products. Consumers have been satisfied with the way in which government regulations have implemented emissions standards in order to ensure that vehicle are operated within the environmental standards. The Home Depot's Eco Options can contribute to firm performance as measured by economic value created through its pricing. If the company establishes prices over the price for production, thus creating a value amount, and then sets the actual price lower to create an actual price that a consumer would be willing to pay, the company would be generating a profit for both the consumer and the company. Accounting profitability and shareholder value, on the other hand, would require that the company demonstrate a consistent competitive advantage over its competitors for a period of time; as the best way to measure a company's shareholder value is through its profitability.

As long as the Home Depot's Eco Options product line continues to generate sales at an accelerated rate and the company continues to produce products of quality and to the consumer's standards, the company could expect a balanced scoreboard that suggests longevity in the market. By using this approach to consistently evaluate company performance with regards to consumer and shareholder opinion, the company can re-establish goals and objective ongoing that address possible deficits before they become a threat to the company's competitive advantage. While the company masters effectiveness regarding the external attributes of its social, ecological, and economic environment, the Home Depot is sure to sustain its strategic advantage in the industry. The Home Depot has successfully incorporated the threats of its external environment by creating a product line that satisfies the demands of its consumers; thus creating an opportunity for generating approval from consumers and shareholders. The act of identifying its strengths and weaknesses in order to better establish goals and objectives that address possible threats to productivity as well as maximize the use of its opportunities, has proven put the company in the best possible position to benefit from the effects of its external environment while utilizing its strengths to overcome its weaknesses. Ford motor company is a multinational company, which has its operations in many countries so the political environment in these countries is very important to the company's operations. The political environment of the major Ford Motor Company markets which includes Japan, Australia, America, and the U.K. are conducive for business operation. These governments are moving toward free economy states hence providing multinationals with good business environments. The economic factors in the external environment are largely macroeconomic and the affect is an economy-wide phenomena. The five macroeconomic factors that firms should consider are growth rates, interest rates, levels of employment, price stability, and currency exchange rates. With the housing market in the doldrums and the economy teetering on recession, Home Depot, the world leading hardware and home improvement retailer had to make some tough decisions. Therefore, Home Depot announced in April, 2007 that it was eliminating 1,200 human resource positions, more than 50 percent of its HR staff. Even in a down economy Home Depot can take advantage of economies of scale due to their immense physical properties. Their huge size makes it difficult for department stores or small retailers to compete on cost and selection.

The global financial crunch has also affected the automobile industry negatively. The current economic environment for Ford Motor Company is difficult but it seems to be recovering. The company needs to adjust to the current economic conditions so it can survive and then make plans to come back during the boom period. This indicates that even though the current economic environment is not conducive, Ford Motor Company can devise strategies that will help to protect it during these difficult times. Also a company wishing to enter the automobile industry requires large scale production facilities and therefore a huge economic commitment so there is little threat of new entrants into the industry.

Sociocultural factors capture a society's cultures, norms, and values. Changing sociocultural factors can create opportunities as well as threats. Many of Home Depot's human resource managers had difficulty adjusting to Home Depot's rough and tumble environment. The result was high attrition and culture clash. Recent changes in the social classes in the world market provides emerging markets in developing economies, which in turn, provides a growing demand for automobiles. This is an opportunity for the Ford Motor Company to expand their market in these countries.

Technological factors capture the application of knowledge to new processes and products. Today's consumers are more aware of fuel consumption and safety standards of their automobiles than ever before. Ford Motor Company should continue to conduct technological research that meets the demands of the consumer. Ecological factors concern broad environmental issues such as the natural environment, global warming, and sustainable economic growth. Consumer awareness about the environment is soaring. Nearly two-thirds (68%) of the world's population is concerned about climate change. Home Depot recently launched a line ecologically friendly products called Eco Options along with a line of energy saving appliances and clean air alternatives. The company also recently launched a print campaign to educate consumers about its green products.

The current strong environmental factor that is affecting the Ford Motor Company is the increased need to reduce the environmental pollution through clean exhaust from motor vehicles. Since Ford Motor Company specializes in the production of motor vehicles, their product offering is limited. Strong ecological forces could possibly hurt the company because it may require a lot of research and innovation to improve their product, all of which could take a huge investment on their part and take a very long time to bring to market. The legal environment captures the official outcomes of the political processes as manifested in laws, mandates, regulations, and court decisions. These in turn can have a direct bearing on a firm's bottom line.

Governments are taking action on greenhouse gas emissions while environmental groups are putting pressure on businesses to clean up their acts. Companies such as Home Depot are realizing they can turn this legal requirement into profit by being more eco-friendly. The major legal factors which Ford Motor Company needs to understand are the labor laws which are ever changing in many countries throughout the world. The labor laws are becoming stricter in different countries requiring good compensation to company workers. This may impact the company operations due to strikes and union pressure. It appears that Home Depot's most important external forces are ecological, sociocultural, and economic and the most important forces for Ford Motor Company would likely be legal, ecological, and economic forces. The forces that impact both companies are economic and ecological. The economy of course affects both companies because if the economy is in a recession and consumers are not purchasing as many products, neither company would be able to sell their products. However, for Home Depot, some DIY projects may actually increase in a down economy. However, this would likely be offset by the reduction in sales of durable goods such as appliance during a recession.

The forces that are different between the two companies are legal and sociocultural. Ford Motor Company may view the legal force with more importance compared to The Home Depot because there are stricter guidelines and regulations for the auto industry than there are for the retail industry. Home Depot may view the sociocultural force more importantly than Ford Motor Company because the type of products Home Depot offers in its retail stores varies depending on its demographics. Customers in different regions have different demands and therefore may influence the type of products Home Depot provides in that particular region. However, I also saw important differences in automobile requirements throughout the world.

Do you believe that The Home Depot is catching the green wave or merely engaging in green-washing (expressing environmentalist concerns as a cover for products, policies, or activities that may not be all that green)/ Support your arguments. By catching the green wave Home Depot saw an opportunity to meet customer demands for more green products and also to improve the planet. They set up strict guidelines for products to earn the Eco Options label. It doesn't take much to convince consumers about the benefits of going green. The evidence about how global warming affects our life every day is there and it feels like its indisputable says Peg Hunter, senior director of marketing at Home Depot. The environment is much more a part of people's psyche and Home Depot wants to be a part of it Consumers are paying for having the product being recognized as green. Even though the product may not have changed there is an additional cost to certify and label that product as eco- friendly which in turn may increase the cost of the product to the consumer. Even though there are some marketers jumping on the environmental bandwagon with one time campaigns, it appears that Home Depot has truly realized that what's good for the earth is actually good for business.

A strong ecological awareness appears to be more of an opportunity for Home Depot than it is for Ford Motor Company because Home Depot can offer eco-friendly products to meet consumer demands/needs relatively easily. This also provides an incentive for suppliers of Home Depot to be innovative and improve their products so they are more ecologically friendly. On the other hand a strong ecological awareness may threaten Ford Motor Company, because if Ford cannot offer more environmentally friendly products to meet consumers' demands/needs they may lose business to their competitors. It is also more expensive and time consuming for Ford Motor Company to develop and offer environmentally friendly products. However, many companies are able to turn threats into opportunities and Home Depot and Ford Motor Company are no exception.

Economic value is created by the Eco Options brand because consumers who demanded "greener" options are more willing to pay a higher price for the Eco Options brand. The Eco Options label can also have a positive effect on accounting profitability and shareholder value if the products do well and generate profits for the shareholders.

Home Depot is making an effort to ensure that in order for
suppliers to earn the Eco Options product label, their
products must meet a strict set of ecologically friendly
guidelines. Home Depot is pushing its suppliers to be more
environmentally sound. The do-it-yourself chain introduced
its Eco Options label in Canada in 2004, and the program
was also recently implemented in the United States. To
qualify for the label, suppliers must answer an extensive
questionnaire that looks at factors such as energy efficiency,
clean air, sustainable forestry, and water efficiency. This can
also help boost their social and ecological performance by
improving their reputation among consumers. It confirms
they are listening to the desires of their customers and
showing that the company cares about the environment by
setting strict criteria for products sold in their stores as
ecologically friendly.

When Home Depot first launched the Eco Options
product label, they were responding to consumers' demands
for green products. This was viewed favorably by consumers
because it showed that Home Depot cared about meeting the
needs and wants of the customer. The more favorable the
consumers' perceptions are, the more likely they are to
purchase the Eco Options products. This could potentially
increase revenues and performance and therefore increase
shareholder satisfaction. This in turn would have a positive
effect on the balanced scorecard. The PESTEL analysis
stands for Political, Economic, Sociocultural, Technological,
Ecological, and Legal factors. The PESTEL model provides a
relatively straightforward way to categorize and analyze the
important external forces that might impinge upon a firm.
Home Depot and Ford Motor Company are both successful
and profitable companies. The PESTEL analysis can be
applied to the Home Depot Company in many ways. For
example, the political activity and government relations
policies are regulated by the federal, state, and local. The
Home Depot combines its vast knowledge of the home
improvement industry with the needs, shopping trends and
customs of each unique geography to best serve customers.
The Home Depot values guide the beliefs and actions of all

associates on a daily basis. The values are the fabric of the Company's unique culture and are central to the success of the Home Depot Company as a whole. Analysis of the Ford Motor Company leads to many of the external forces impinging upon the company as the Home Depot Company. The Ford Motor Company shows its commitment to innovation in outstanding fuel economy, head-turning style, and customer-focused technology. Both of these companies are customer-based and innovation to the style and changes to the customer as an individual and whole.

I believe that Home Depot is "catching the green wave" too and for the public and as for corporate contributions to the very important issues in today's society. The Home Depot Company is actively involved in pursuing environmental excellence through their stores and vendors. They are dedicated to making communities a better place for generations to come. From the Environmental Principles, Environmental Milestones, Customer Education Programs, Recycling, and Corporate Contributions, it is clearly stated the Home Depot Company puts the efforts, time and interest to the public and consumer as an individual.

I do not believe it is ethical to charge a price premium for "green label products" even through some of them were already offered and the only change is that they now carry a "green label." I do not think it is a profitable idea because the possibility of the consumer knowing this will turn heads away especially is they are more of a "smart shopper" than just the consumer who needs the product immediately and last minute. In today's economy, the "smart shopper" will have done his/her homework and visited several weekly advertisements through newspaper, media, etc. and light bulbs tend to go off in a sense to go where it is less expensive. Word of mouth advertising would not be popular to the business of the store itself, and possibly to all other locations of the stores.

After reviewing the SWOT (Strengths Weaknesses Opportunities Threats) analysis in comparison to The Home Depot Company and The Ford Motor Company, The Home Depot Company has the strength in the ecological environment regarding cleaning products, appliances, lawn care and equipment, and energy savers for the home. A possible weakness for The Home Depot Company would not have their products backed up by the federal, state and local government's rules and regulations. The Ford Motor Company has a threat to the ecological environment in regard to the building of the exhaust system and fuel lines on new and used vehicles. There are opportunities for The Ford Motor Company to always enhance and improve better exhaust systems and cleaner engines for the air quality and environment as a whole. Companies can turn threats into opportunities by considering additional resources and capabilities that may be needed in order to take advantage of these external opportunities and mitigate threats.

The Home Depot Company Eco Options can be a significant positive contributor to firm performance as measured by economic value created, accounting profitability, and shareholder value. Economic value is evaluated for any good or service that a firm offers in the marketplace, such as value, cost, and price. The accounting profitability for The Home Depot Company would be the financial statements and income statements in particular; the numbers showing a profit from the Eco Options programs that have been developed and profited from over a time period. The shareholder value is the measure of competitive advantage that matters most is the return on their risk capital. What the shareholder(s) have invested and the return on risk capital, including stock price appreciation plus dividends received over a specific period of time. Another issue to consider is the Balanced Scorecard for the Eco Options. The Balanced Scorecard is an approach that harnesses multiple internal and external performance metrics in order to balance both financial and strategic goals.

Four key questions to ask and answer are: How do customers view us? How do we create value? What core competencies do we need?, And How do shareholders view us? Finally, the Triple Bottom Line is a combination of economic, social, and ecological concerns that can lead to a sustainable strategy. Economic, social, and ecological are three dimensions that make up the triple bottom line. Achieving results in all three areas can lead to a sustainable energy. In conclusion to the demand for an ecological environment, The Home Depot Company, The Ford Motor Company, and Eco Option programs, I think that the individual consumer needs to do more research on what is Eco friendly products and services, how the consumer can make it a better place to live, and for the consumer to be better informed about Eco Options in today's society. The Home Depot has launched their line of Eco Options products comprised of biodegradable materials. Some products have an up-charge for wearing that logo and it may be viewed as an unethical practice. After all, how are we supposed to help to save the planet if the increased prices for Eco Options products are raising thus creating roadblocks? Eco Options products should be marked down and made easier for everyone to purchase thus strengthening the movement. For now, The Home Depot is seeing increased profits from their new branding strategy and is taking moderate steps towards improving their product selection.

The PESTEL framework organizes external forces in to categories. It is an acronym for Political, Economic, Socio-Cultural, Technological, Ecological and Legal external environments. Political influences come from government bodies that influence company decisions. The economic influences need to be considered on a macro level such as interest rates, growth rates (good and services produced in our economy), levels of employment, inflation, deflation and exchange rates. Low interest rates will have a direct bearing on increased consumer spending and high levels of employment will signify that a firm will have to pay more to get a quality employee, as resources are scarce. Socio-cultural mixed with ecological factors are the ones Home Depot is facing due to the overwhelming trend in consumers' concern of global warming and wanting to make a difference. Technological factors simply let us know whether a business should consider a larger online presence or focus more on their technological appeal. Ford is also facing socio-cultural and ecological environment changes in addition to technological. Just like with Home depot, customers are looking for the new electric cars because they are good for the environment and the new cool thing to have. With electric cars comes a lot more technology thus changing the approach to building a car the typical way. Out with combustible chambers and gasoline and in with electric, emission free, clean engines.

After further reading, I believe that The Home Depot and giants like them are mostly capitalizing on the trend. They are, however, carrying products from companies that truly do care about the environment and make a difference. So The Home Depot is a vessel so smaller companies that actually do care about the environment can get their name out and donate to the cause even is large retailers don't care as much. The only reason a company would do such a thing was to capitalize on the current trend of "buying green". Eco friendly products should save people money and be enticing to purchase to accelerate their positive effect on the environment. With their prices rising and companies cashing in they are creating speed bumps for customers especially considering the current economic situation. People are more prone to buy cheap than quality thus many times omitting the more expensive eco-friendly products.

Both The Home Depot and Ford are facing ecological awareness threats but I believe that the threat is greater for Ford. There are more substitutes for ford then there are for The Home Depot. Ford is the product whereas. The Home Depot is a retailer that is fairly unique in what it can offer to the customer. Ford along with many other car manufacturers had to file bankruptcy and they cannot afford to do it again. The product offering in The Home Depot is so large that even if their eco-friendly idea flops they will retain many customers because they offer items that many handy men and builders simply cannot do without and don't care whether it's eco-friendly or not. A threat of can be turned into an opportunity by cornering the market by partnering with eco certifying groups and offering a good deal for a quality product to the customer. Whether it is a car or a random product, this approach will work. It can even help to re-invent and improve many aspects and make them even more eco-friendly than before.

The Home Depot

	Positive	Negative
Internal factors	**Strengths** • Strong brand • Great product selection • Convenient locations • Open 7 days a week	**Weakness** • Large retailer reduced credibility • Not all eco-friendly items approved
External factors	**Opportunity** • Ensure that all eco-friendly items are approved • Partner with eco-friendly groups to provide and receive guidance • Lower prices on eco-friendly goods to aid in protecting the environment	**Threat** • Other large retailers jumping on board • Smaller companies gaining recognition with quality products • Readily available real eco-friendly products online • Smaller companies exposing "eco-friendly" sales tactics of large retailers.

	Positive	Negative
Internal factors	**Strengths** • Great brand name • Lots of resources • Large R&D • American made product	**Weakness** • Poor history of reliability • Inferior product from imports • Poor product quality • Doesn't easily mold to customer needs

	Opportunity	Threat
External factors	• Re-invest in R&D to increase quality • Create reliable and quality electric cars • Regain American quality product appearance	• Foreign manufacturers are already ahead of the game with electric cars • New smaller car companies saturating the market • Inability to escape previous failures and quality control

All off these options will have a positive outcome considering the recent socio-ecological trends in culture and in the industry. Customers are willing to pay a premium therefore the return on investment will increase. There will be a positive impact seen in the triple bottom line as even though the Eco friendly brand may not be 100% certified most products sold are donating to the overall good of the environment which correlates with being socially responsible. Social responsibility and good publicity leads to increased profits. The strategic alignment of the company with what they are doing now in congruence with their financial, learning, internal and customer goals will benefit. Perhaps they aren't perfect yet in their Eco friendly line of products but it may be a work in progress as the movement catches on.

PESTEL is an acronym that stands for P - Political, E-Economic, S - Socio-cultural, T Technological, E - Ecological, and L- Legal. PESTEL is used to assess the impact of external factors on a firm. These forces are embedded in the global environment and create both opportunities and threats, so it pays to monitor them closely. The most important external factors affecting Home Depot would be the ecological and socio-cultural. In this case study they are primarily concerned with targeting the market that is concerned with the environment. This is why the created the ECO options line.

Ford is also affected by the socio-cultural to make more

earth friendly fueling options for their vehicles. However, I feel they have a lot more legal, political, and technological externals factors to be concerned with because of their close ties to the oil industry. The oil industry itself is heavily regulated and co-dependent on political and economic factors. Ford also has to be on top of the technological factor to stay on the cutting edge of technology for their vehicles.

I believe like any company, Home Depot is concerned in making a profit. However, their Eco Options line do meet some strict standards: Sustainable Forestry, Clean Air, Water Conservation, Energy Efficient, and Healthy Home. So regardless of whether they are going green just to make a buck, they have encouraged vendors to become more eco-friendly because that is popular with their consumer. So regardless of their true intentions, I believe their eco-line is in line with the "green wave" because the market is demanding some changes and they are willing to pay for them.

I understand that when some companies truly go green with their manufacturing, it may cost them more to produce their product. In this case, I think a reasonably adjusted price for the cost of manufacturing green would be legitimate. However, when the product did not change and they merely raise the price because it has a green label on it, then I would have doubts in regards to ethics. Although if the new packaging was triggering a rise in demand, I believe in the free market and when demand goes up, prices will go up. So at some point, I believe it would be price gouging, but I'm not sure this is the case at Home Depot. I would need a little more information to make a truly strong statement either way.

When you look at these for Home Depot and Ford, I believe that a stronger ecological awareness by the consumer is a threat for Ford because of their dependence on gasoline. They have a much tougher market for competition when it comes to creating vehicles that get better gas mileage and are more eco-friendly to the environment. Home Depot on the other hand, is taking that awareness and turning it into an opportunity by capitalizing on that market. They created a product line, ECO Options to target that market and profit by their awareness.

However just because the Eco-aware consumer can be a threat to FORD, they could certainly turn that threat into an opportunity. If they also create a product line (vehicle), that is more fuel-efficient and earth friendly than their competitors, they could capitalize on that niche consumer just like Home Depot is doing. You can take any firms performance of a product and plug it into any of the three systems above. If the product is truly profitable, it can be measured regardless of which model you use to measure it. The balanced scorecard would be my first choice because this approach "harnesses multiple internal and external performance metrics in order to balance both financial and strategic goals. This method seems like it would be a natural and logical fit for what Home Depot is trying to accomplish with their ECO Options line.

The Home Depot's Eco Options Boost Profit Margins. The book discussed the growing demand from consumers for more green products and Home Depot's reaction to this demand shift and the outcome. This book serves to analyze the implications of Home Depot's Eco Options label and its impact on the firm/industry. This book discussed Home Depots new label, Eco Options and the success that it has seen since its launch on Earth Day 2007. This new label garnered an 85 percent price premium and brought in about $2.2 billion in sales. The brand continues to grow fast and has even sparked the launch of similar lines with competitors. Also, the desire to earn an Eco Options label from the Home Depot has spurred its suppliers to modernize by offering even more ecologically friendly products, such as super low-flow toilets and energy-efficient appliances and lighting.

A firm's macro environment consists of a wide range of political, economic, sociocultural, technological, ecological, and legal (PESTEL) factors that an affect industry and firm performance. A company like Home Depot has to be hyper-aware of these factors as they sell a variety of products that have various repercussions. Consider the implications of these factors and what actions a manager need to employ in order to seize opportunities or nullify threats. Companies like The Home Depot and Ford Motor Company need to pay extra attention to ecological factors as they concern broad environmental issues such as natural environment, global warming and sustainable economic growth.

Both Home Depot and Ford Motor Companies manufacture and/or sell products that have a significant impact on the environment (vehicle emissions, energy-efficient transportation, biodegradable products, home appliances, etc.), and they need to monitor the performance of their products and the impact they resonate. Although a company like Ford deals with alternate fuel sources and lowering emissions while Home Depot deals more with sustainable forestry, energy conservation/efficiency, and water conservation – they are both facing the same challenging forces when trying to cater to the environment. Interestingly, by creating products that are more "green," these firms are also increasing their technology and encouraging suppliers to innovate.

Possible problems of this green wave are that consumers are trusting companies to tell them what is and is not environmentally friendly. The only way a customer knows that one type of mulch may injure their pet and another won't is by the labeling. Home Depot created their Eco Options brand and the specifications necessary to obtain that label. Really how much better is that product than its non-green counterpart? Aside from doing scientific research and educating myself on reading chemical labels, I will have to take Home Depot's word for it. Perhaps if the company educated people more about what it takes to earn the Eco Options label, they could increase sales even further.

Home Depot appears to be making a legitimate effort and is "catching the green wave" because they have seen how these products garner an 85 percent price premium and have brought them billions in revenue since their launch in 2007. Home Depot was ingenious with the strategy to award suppliers with the brand, thereby encouraging them to create even more products and selections that will help Home Depot's overall image. It is difficult for a company to go green: the recession, coupled with the typically higher costs of green practices and products for organizations and consumers and inefficient or reduced business tax credits and incentives for green technologies and building design, has slowed the green wave's advance. With this in mind, it is very clear that Home Depot is not simply engaging in "green washing" and recognized going green as a positive intangible resource.

It is important for Home Depot to monitor the resource flow of their green products to make sure that they are getting a positive return on investment (ROI). If they are selling enough units, the brand will be profitable. Even if they are not selling enough units they may still keep the brand(s) because it provides them with positive press and can attract more customers just because it is there. As we know, price is based off of demand. I think that the products should be priced based on their manufacturing and shipping costs, however that is not how business is conducted. Any company will find the equilibrium price point where they can maximize price and sell the most units.

Conducting a SWOT analysis of Home Depot will reveal the following information: Strengths – great customer service, loyal customers, strong brand equity, and great growth history, Weaknesses – stores are not aesthetically pleasing, bad communication, no online presence, and not innovative, Opportunities – could improve store aesthetics, online presence, acquisitions, and innovation, and Threats – Lowe's seems to be catching up, economic slowdown, lower cost competitors or imports, and economic slowdown.

Home Depot has some great areas of opportunity to expand their green movement and bring even more positive attention to their firm. A complete revamping of the stores aesthetics could also showcase the use of many of the green products and Eco Options brand. This will illustrate their commitment to going green and having a positive impact on the environment. In this evolving period of economic growth, organizations that succeed in creating and retaining this type of learning culture, that support their leaders' SWOT, and follow through with required actions will have a significant competitive advantage over those that don't.

Home Depot has created additional economic value for their stores and products with the launch of the Eco Options brand. This line has also encouraged their suppliers to innovate their products to earn the label, thereby providing Home Depot locations with even more green products. This line has brought them about $2.2 billion and is continuing to grow, offering more opportunities for the firm.

The strategic group, in essence, consists of the firm's closest competitors. Just outside the strategic group is the industry in which the company operates. The industries differ along important structural dimensions such as the number and the size of competitors in an industry and the type of products or services offered. The industries that are in turn are embedded in the larger macro environment, in which a wide variety of focus exert their influence.

Support your arguments. Competitor Lowe's was also quick to cash the green wave. Early in 2007, it began introducing organic gardening supplies, including fertilizer, soil, and insecticides that are not only ecologically friendly but also harmless for the children and pets Lowes claims that more than 100 million people in the United States use some kind of organic lawn and garden product.

Organic foods—which consumers buy more for their own health than for the environment's—accounted for less than 3 percent of all food sales in 2006, according to the *Nutrition Business Journal*. In 2006, green laundry detergents and household cleaners made up less than 2 percent of sales in their categories. And despite their trendiness, hybrid cars made up little more than 2 percent of the U.S. auto market in 2007, according to a report by J.D. Power and Associates.

As a result, consumers in the United States and other developed countries have done little to lighten their carbon footprints. Some of this lags between talking and walking could reflect consumers' insincerity, laziness, posturing, or other unsavory traits. But much more of it is because businesses have not educated consumers about the benefits of green products and have failed to create green products that meet consumers' needs.

Consumers want to act green, but they expect businesses to lead the way. According to our global survey, 61 percent of consumers say that corporations should take the lead in tackling the issue of climate change. To do this, businesses need to develop more and better Earth-friendly products. Some already are, but they are not doing a good job of marketing them, finds a Climate Group study, which discovered that two-thirds of American and British consumers cannot name a green brand. Similarly, the 2007 National Technology Readiness Survey of 1,025 U.S. adults found that more than two thirds of participants say they prefer to do business with environmentally responsible companies, but almost half say it is difficult to find green goods and services.

SWOT analysis is designed to help identify several areas of a business that may need improvement and other areas where the company may be able to improve upon. SWOT is an acronym for; Strength, Weakness, Opportunities and Threats. A company should consider this analysis to be one of the most important steps to becoming one of the leading stores and schools of this nature in the area. A business idea gets started by acquiring knowledge of a product, market or skill. In this case, the company's idea got started from the skills gained from years of diving and love of water and marine life. These things inspired the owner to start his business. One of the most difficult things to identify as a business owner and as an entrepreneur is that area where the company or owner is lacking strength. When considering a business venture, normally one is not looking at the negative factors of the business itself. In most cases, the entrepreneur looks at the positive factors that can help his business get started.

SWOT Analysis: Strengths (1) Highly Qualified Staff, (2) Reasonable Prices, (3) Over 20 years' experience in the business, (4) Offers safety training, certifications, and (5)

Good rapport with customers. Weaknesses: (1) Lack of mission statement on the website, (2) Lack of competition, Limited funds (Typical in small businesses), and (3) Over millions of dollars in inventory (Too much capital invested in inventory). Opportunities: (1) Virtual store (Offering used equipment and possible equipment trade-in), (2) New retail store (3) Proper advertisement (Direct mail, sponsorships, place mats, radio, television advertisement, travel and sports magazines, Verizon yellow book etc.), (4) Better use of database (Identify professionals, use of ACT database), (5) Educational level (Educate customers/Non-credit courses through a College), and (6) Dive salvage business (Introduction letter and direct mail to local insurance adjusters). Threats: (1) Internet competition, (2) Economic downturn (Disposable income), (3) Limited area of exposure (Limited to surrounding areas), and (4) Possible stealing (How to reduced that). Being a more ecologically minded company is becoming more important to how consumer view your company. They are many ways for a company to become more ecologically friendly. This can be done through the products they sell or buy. Home Depot has seen the opportunity that is the green movement and has joined.

Home Depot saw that there was a growing concern among its buyers for more ecologically friendly products. They launched a product label that was ecologically friendly in five ways: sustainable energy, clean air, water conservation, energy efficient, and healthy home. Home Depot suppliers responded by offering products that would fit the new label and customers showed their support in buying 2.2 billion dollars' worth giving the new Eco Option label a 85 percent price premium. Home Depot direct competitor Lowes was quick to see the competitive advantage and produced their own eco-friendly products. In analyzing PESTEL factors effecting both Home Depot and Ford Motor Company I found some factors that are the same in both groups specifically those concerning the change to be more ecologically friendly.

There are political factors that are changing how much carbon can be produced by a company and by automobiles. Quotas for how much clean energy is used and how many cars are using alternative fuels are being set by the government. The Federal Trade Commission issues Green Guides that specifies what the guidelines are for making environment–related marketing claims. Both Ford and Home Depot will need to be in compliance on their eco - friendly claims they make about their products. There are also tax incentives to use green products or clean energy.

Economic factors are affecting both Ford and Home Depot when it comes to clean energy. Home Depot has seen an increase in sales and an 85 percent premium in sales of Eco friendly labels. Ford has also seen a difference in the growth rates of different models of vehicles. They are selling more alternative fuel vehicles using electricity for a power source. They are selling more vehicles that have better fuel efficiency. There is a growing market for all kinds of eco-friendly products from cars to fertilizer.

Being eco-friendly has become a culture movement. Studies have found that 36 percent of hybrid cars were sold to buyers that bought them because they wanted to have a visibly green vehicle. The push for being green is all over with all types of products and ideas are being offered. People are becoming more conscious of the pollution and waste that is happening and want to do something to limit their footprint. It can be from water conservative showerheads to hybrid cars.

There has been large growth in electronic vehicle technology. All types of clean energy technology have developed. Home Depot sells items that use the technology to make more economically friendly products such as light bulbs and toilets that have been redesigned to be more efficient and use less energy or water. Concerns for global warming and evidence of practices that lead to it are increasing. Water, oil, and other natural recourses are being used up at a rate that is not sustainable. There are concerns about the safety of nuclear power because of the problems in Japan after an earthquake and tsunami. These fears lead to Ford making hybrids and more fuel efficient vehicles. Home Depot is looking for more options for using recycled products.

Laws are being passed for products to be required to be ecologically friendly. It can be as specific to the chemicals used to clean your car. Home Depot needs to be aware of these laws on what types of products they can carry. The same for Ford, the new laws on what types of chemicals that can be used will affect the products they produce and sell. In many ways the PESTEL analysis has similar concerns for both Home Depot and Ford. The green movement is a growing cultural movement that needs to be analyses and decision on how the company will respond to the new external factor needs to be addressed.

I believe that Home Depot is working to catch the green wave. The Green Guide helps keep a company being more honest on what they are labeling eco-friendly. Just green washing would be short term strategy that could cause problems with bad publicity if the products were found to not live up to the claims that Home Depot was making. I do not believe that Home Depot wants to take the risk with their brand by using false advertising to build hype about their green products. It would have detrimental long term effects.

If the product was already being sold at one price and nothing changed but the label I do not think it would be ethical to charge more for the product just because of a label change. It would be ethical to change more for a green product than a regular one if it cost more to produce. It is not costing the company more to produce the product they are just taking advantage of peoples' desire to be more ecologically responsible this is unethical behavior.

When using a SWOT analysis in looking at Ford and Home Depot I see that the green movement is an opportunity for both companies to expand into. Home Depot has already found it can bring in revenue and has started as a market leader in is industry. Ford is not as well placed to take advantage of being greener. Its weakness is the difficultly of switching the type of fuel people use to run their vehicles. The infrastructure is not yet built to support electric cars the way gas stations are available. I think Ford will find the ecological awareness a threat more than Home Depot who will see more opportunity. Ford could turn the threat into an opportunity if they can develop better hybrid technology or find a way to match up with a gas company such as Shell to offer electric car power options as well as fuel.

Home Depot can be a positive contributor to economic value by offering eco-friendly products that customers are willing to pay higher prices for. This increase in revenue helps accounting profitability. Over all the company has a new area to grow in helping shareholder value. The triple bottom dimensions of economic, social, and ecological will all benefit from have the eco-friendly products. Eco friendly products help the company's balanced scorecard buy changing how customers view the company. It can help customers have a positive view of the direction Home Depot is going and build their brand and loyalty in their customers. It can also show that they are creating value in providing more ecologically friendly products this helps them be a better socially motivated company.

The Home Depot has stood up to the challenge of addressing the consumer demands for a diverse range of products that are ecologically made with the maintenance of the environment in mind. As a result, the company launched its Eco Options line that specifically targeted those products in response; thus, transforming and external treat into an opportunity for profitability. The Ford Motor Company's implementation of manufacturing electric vehicles is another example of how a company is able to maintain its competitive advantage by creating goals and objectives that addresses external threats by utilizing the company's internal strengths in order to generate opportunity.

The external forces impinging upon the Home Depot and the Ford Motor Co. are different as the Home Depot has been imposed by ecological and socio-cultural attributes and the Ford Motor Co. is affected by external forces that are political with a combination of technological and economical attributes. As Home Depot responded to consumer's demands for more green products, in response, Home Depot launched a new product label called Eco Options that designated products within its supple as ecologically friendly. With Home Depot's suppliers wanting to be included in this specialized line of products, interested suppliers developed more innovative ways to incorporate its products. The Eco Options brand makes it easy for consumers to recognize products that make a difference, one choice at a time. Every product with the Eco Options label has less of an impact on the environment than competing products. Specifically, Eco Options products offer one or more of the following benefits: Energy Efficiency, Water Conservation, Healthy Home, Clean Air, and Sustainable Forestry. These items included super low-flow toilets and energy efficient appliances and lighting, thus Home Depot initiating the ecological phenomenon in home improvement.

Home Depot was affected by the socio-cultural affects externally due to consumer demands for Eco friendly products. With these consumers having a culture that is sensitive to the affects that products may have on the environment, Home Depot incorporated these concerns in its marketing plan by developing and launching the Eco Options product label. As the community of consumers, for which the Home Depot services, lives a lifestyle congruent with values that are concerned with environmental awareness, developing such line as Eco Options demonstrates Home Depot's response to its external socio-culture atmosphere.

With regards to the Ford Motor Co., the political and economic external effects were most impinging. As Ford, GM, and Chrysler maintained a monopoly in the automobile industry for most of the 20th century, the foreign competitors intensified competition while threatening Ford's market shares. To address the political consequences on development once imposed, these foreign entities built U.S. plants in order to evade import restrictions. Ford was also affected economically due to the expense of the production of its product as the company needed to manufacture its fleet on a larger scale. As a result of this imposition of cost, Ford began to generate its own electric vehicles. Providing electrification technologies is a key component of Ford's broader strategy of producing vehicles that have improved fuel economy and diminished greenhouse emissions. Due to a consumer demand for more technological innovations; electric vehicles have become more prevalent.

It is undetermined at this time whether or not the Home Depot has caught the "Green Wave" or is "Green washing". If the company fails to expand within the community in order to assist with the overall transition to a more environment conscious lifestyle for all citizens, it could be believed that it is simply capitalizing on the consumer's demand for more Ego friendly products, thus generating income. Merely establishing a line of products that target the need to address the preservation of the environment isn't a demonstration of a true depiction of a company's value towards the issue.

It is not ethical to charge an increased price for the Eco friendly products if these products do not warrant this increase due to an increase in expense to acquire from the manufacturer. However, if the increase in price included an established amount to be donated to the cause for improving the environment, and such donation was equal to the difference between the original and escalated price, then such increase is warranted. Creating an elevated price for these specialized products would suggest that the consumers who are expected to purchase these items are targeted and discriminated against because of its preference.

The SWOT analysis could be used to determine which of the two companies, the Home Depot or the Ford Motor Co., has a stronger ecological awareness by consumers as a threat and as an opportunity. It appears that the Home Depot is threatened more by the ecological awareness of consumers as it attempts to sell products that have the potential to damage the environment. However, it appears that the company has turned the threat into an opportunity by developing the Eco Options line of earth friendly products. The Ford Motor Company is less threatened by this same consumer awareness, as consumers are less demanding of vehicles that maintain environmental quality than their demand for home improvement products. Consumers have been satisfied with the way in which government regulations have implemented emissions standards in order to ensure that vehicle are operated within the environmental standards.

The Home Depot's Eco Options can contribute to firm performance as measured by economic value created through its pricing. If the company establishes prices over the price for production, thus creating a value amount, and then sets the actual price lower to create an actual price that a consumer would be willing to pay, the company would be generating a profit for both the consumer and the company. Accounting profitability and shareholder value, on the other hand, would require that the company demonstrate a consistent competitive advantage over its competitors for a period of time; as the best way to measure a company's shareholder value is through its profitability.

As long as the Home Depot's Eco Options product line continues to generate sales at an accelerated rate and the company continues to produce products of quality and to the consumer's standards, the company could expect a balanced scoreboard that suggests longevity in the market. By using this approach to consistently evaluate company performance with regards to consumer and shareholder opinion, the company can re-establish goals and objective ongoing that address possible deficits before they become a threat to the company's competitive advantage. While the company masters effectiveness regarding the external attributes of its social, ecological, and economic environment, the Home Depot is sure to sustain its strategic advantage in the industry.

The Home Depot has successfully incorporated the threats of its external environment by creating a product line that satisfies the demands of its consumers; thus creating an opportunity for generating approval from consumers and shareholders. The act of identifying its strengths and weaknesses in order to better establish goals and objectives that address possible threats to productivity as well as maximize the use of its opportunities, has proven put the company in the best possible position to benefit from the side effects of its external environment while utilizing its strengths to overcome its weaknesses.

CHAPTER 7
IKEA Inc.

The Wonder from Sweden: Is IKEA's Success Sustainable? The world's most successful global retailer, in terms of profitability, is not Walmart or the French grocery chain Carrefour, but IKEA-a home-furnishings company from Sweden. In 2010, IKEA had more than 310 stores worldwide in 38 countries, employed some 127,000 people, and earned revenues of 32 billion euros. More than 80 percent of IKEA's revenues come from Europe, with the rest from North America (16 percent) and Asia and Australia (3 percent). This paper will seek to answer whether or not this kind growth is sustainable.

As things stand, IKEA's greatest threats seem to be both internal and external. The first threat to further expansion would be the problem with finding an alternative supply of source materials to replace wood. The next threat might be the fact that the company is still being controlled by an aging founder that must be consulted on every company decision. The final threat seems to be the fact that the company is held through a complicated network of foundations and holding companies.

According to latest reports from Bloomberg.com, IKEA is ultimately owned by a Dutch trust controlled by the Kamprad family, with various holding companies handling different aspects of IKEA's operations, such as franchising, manufacturing, and distribution. As for the supply factor problem, it would seem that IKEA has adopted a go-green corporate strategy. According to an article by Jasmine G. entitled, Ikea: Affordable and Environmentally Friendly? The international manufacturer has set an admirable standard for others to follow because of its commitment to sustainability. The IKEA way outlines corporate responsibility for waste, emissions and the handling of chemicals. Third-party auditors complete over 1,000 audits a year to ensure that all of its suppliers are following the guidelines. These audits are also done for all of IKEA's wood suppliers to make sure that all meet the minimum requirement that includes no illegally harvested trees, no harvesting in uncertified intact forests and no GM trees. IKEA's aim is to have at least 35 percent of its suppliers become Forest Stewardship Counsel certified.

We all learn that both a developed country (the United States) and also emerging economies (i.e., China and Russia) are the fastest growing international markets for IKEA.

The fact that IKEA is competitive in both markets is not surprising when one considers IKEA's ability to establish relationships with key suppliers in the markets that they enter. On the other hand, IKEA did face quite a challenge in China according an article from businesstoday.com. In China, however, IKEA faced strange problems. Its low-price approach created misunderstanding among ambitious Chinese consumers while local competitors copied its designs. However, IKEA overcame most of their issues by forming a joint venture which served as a good platform to test the market, understand local needs, and adapt its strategies accordingly. The company faced similar problems in the United States and had to customize its products based on local needs. IKEA's new strategy to compete globally will include a new sustainability strategy designed to help the company become energy independent by 2020. The new strategy will be realized through its "People and Planet Positive" plan which aims to convert all of its traditional lighting to LED lighting which uses up to 85 percent less electricity and has a lifespan of 20 years, and this the company hopes to have completed by 2016.

Long-term plans for the company also includes becoming energy and resource independent by "securing long-term access to sustainable raw materials, promoting recycling and using resources within the limits of the planet." IKEA currently has a $1.8 billion allocated for its wind and solar projects for its wind farms located in six European countries along with 342,000 solar panels installed in stores. In addition, IKEA will be looking to boost sustainability among suppliers by encouraging them to focus on compliance and shared values. IKEA will accomplish this by extending a code of conduct through its value chain. It's important to have the supply chain follow the company's overarching standards. We are informed that in most cases, sustainability creates efficiencies, thus saving money and creating new business opportunities.

I would recommend that IKEA do its best to achieve corporate social responsibility and business ethics. If the company decides to focus on *corporate social responsibility*, then the practice of good *business ethics* would be a natural outcome. According to a CSR Press Release in September, 2012, IKEA was lauded for the state of Connecticut's largest solar array in New Haven. The article went on to state that IKEA now surpasses a 70% solar presence on its U.S. locations. The IKEA New Haven store installation will consist of an 118,000-square-foot PV array consisting of a 940.8-kW system, built with 3,920 panels. According to IKEA New Haven store manager Gail Franc, I want you to know that the mission of IKEA is the subsequent, our mission is to create a better everyday life for many people and IKEA, and we just added to this effort. A solar energy system will assist to reduce the store's carbon footprint and epitomizes another investment toward our future in every community. IKEA believes it can be an excellent business while conducting good business and aims to curtail impacts on the environment. Globally, IKEA assesses locations regularly for safeguarding opportunities, incorporates innovative materials into product design, works to preserve sustainable resources, and flat-packs goods for efficient distribution.

Although IKEA has become known as one of the most profitable companies in the Home Furnishings Industry in Europe, it has not mastered that goal within the United States due to the competiveness of Target and Wal-Mart. In order to conquer this challenge, the company must devise a plan that addresses how the company will manufacture products with alternative materials than wood and do so at the lowest possible cost to the company. With environmentalists concern about the condition of our forest due to trees being sacrificed for furnishings, IKEA needs to take heed to these concerns and find a way to deviate from wood being its main source of supply. With Ikea's fastest growing market being in the United States, China, and Russia, the company's largest market remains within Germany. Although it took the company nearly 20 years to expand beyond the boundaries of Sweden, Ikea implemented its international strategy by expanding first to Europe and then beyond to the United States. Through its international plan, the company was able to market its products that it was already successfully selling in its home industry to an industry international without having to adapt its product to accommodate the new market. While focusing on value and low cost, Ikea has "endeavored to accomplish economies of scale through administering a global supply chain such as Russia as a key source of supply due to wood being one of Ikea's main raw material.

While maintaining the position as the world's most profitable source of quality and affordable home furnishings, Ikea experienced several external challenges such as finding new sources of supply to support more store openings, the effects of society's sensitivity towards the destruction of wood (which is Ikea's main input factor) which is associated with the concern for global warming, and the need to find a low cost replacement for wood. Although the American market presents as a growing industry influenced by Ikea, the company holds only 5 percent of the home furnishings market. To keep Ikea at bay, Target Company has currently recruited exemplary designers and inaugurated a wide range of low-priced furnishings. Kmart, likewise, has hired Martha Stewart to assist with the design of its offerings of home furnishings.

The greatest threat to the company appears to be that of the external threat of the challenge of finding new sources of supply to accommodate an increase in store openings. Not having the supply available to accommodate the demand of products needed by its consumers can cause the company to suffer its patrons seeking products from its competitors due to a lack of supply. In order to alleviate this possibility, IKEA should immediately find way to manufacture its products with vendors that can provide a large return of products as well find other materials to substitute for the wood concern.

As it is not surprising to learn that the United States as well as China and Russia is ones of the fastest growing international markets for IKEA, there is a possible challenge in the way IKEA should compete across the globe. With companies such as Wal-Mart, Target, and Home Goods making it difficult for IKEA to assume and maintain leverage within the home furnishings industry, IKEA needs to develop a plan that addresses the limited supply of materials, keeping in mind the community concern for the environment, as well as cost effectiveness. I am convinced that prefabricated construction is respected by many people as an effective and efficient strategy to improving construction processes and productivity, ensuring product quality and minimizing time and cost in the industry. However, several problems transpire with this strategy in practice, including higher risk levels and cost or time overruns. In order to resolve such difficulties, it is proposed that the IKEA model of the manufacturing industry and VP technology are introduced into a prefabricated construction process. The concept of the IKEA model is acknowledged in detail and VP technology is briefly introduced. In combination with VP technology, the uses of the IKEA model are presented in detail, i.e. design optimization, production optimization and installation optimization. Furthermore, through a case study of a prefabricated hotel project in Hong Kong, it is shown that the VP-based IKEA model can improve the efficiency and safety of prefabricated construction as well as decreasing cost and time. In fact, IKEA is faced with many challenges regarding its ability to gain a better competitive advantage against its competitors within the home furnishings industry. Once it solves the major problem of how it plans to manufacture materials used to fabricate its products, it could possibly place itself at the head of the pack when it comes to the home furnishings industry.

Dr. Ebenezer A. Robinson, PhD

8 CHAPTER NAME
Infosys Inc.

Adrian Patel (managing partner), has been tasked with helping the company gain a strategic advantage in the competitive U.S. IT consulting market, despite the current backlash against outsourcing U.S. jobs to foreign workers. Adrian must determine the most serious threats (foreign competitors, Indian competitors, changes in U.S. and/or Indian tax codes, the H-1B visa debate) facing Infosys Consulting and formulate an appropriate strategic response. How can the company plan for growth in such an uncertain external environment, and where should it get the human resources to support its growth objectives?

The case begins as Adrian Patel (managing partner) returns from Infosys's Annual Strategy Retreat at the company headquarters in Bangalore, India. Adrian has been tasked with helping the company gain a strategic advantage in the competitive U.S. IT consulting market, despite the current backlash against outsourcing U.S. jobs to foreign workers. Politicians have been threatening to end tax incentives to U.S. companies that create jobs overseas, as well as limit the H-1B visa program that companies use to bring skilled foreign technical workers to the United States. These changes would constitute a significant blow to Infosys's business model, which relies on the ability to source technology work from wherever high-quality talent is available at a cost-competitive rate.

Infosys was founded in Pune, India, by N. R. Murthy and six friends in July 1981 (it later relocated to Bangalore). Because India lacked an established software development industry, the company focused on the United States market from the beginning. Initial growth was slow due to extensive governmental red tape in India, and the company nearly collapsed when U.S.-based Kurt Salmon Associates terminated its joint venture with Infosys in 1989. However, Indian economic reform in the 1990s lifted many of the regulations that had stagnated development, launching a period of rapid expansion. Infosys went public on the Indian stock exchange in 1993, and later became the first Indian company to be listed (on NASDAQ) in the United States. Today, Infosys is one of the world's leading IT service firms with annual revenues nearing $5 billion and a presence in more than 30 countries; its North American operations account for 68 percent of overall sales.

The Obama administration has proposed policies to encourage companies to move back to the United States, while closing corporate tax loopholes that make it easier for multinationals to pay limited taxes on their overseas operations. Some Democratic lawmakers, along with union representatives, believe Obama's proposals will help address a weak job market and troubling budget deficits. But Republicans, some Democrats, and industry representatives fear higher taxes on U.S.-based multinationals will lead to an exodus of business, investment, and jobs. Yet even as Congressional Democrats and Republicans introduced competing bills this month to increase high-skilled immigration, the Obama administration is preparing to implement regulations that will restrict the visa process. Worse, administration documents revealed last week that since 2008, officials failed to issue thousands of legally-required high-skilled visas.

Recent U.S. jobs reports were bleak at best driving down the hopes of a robust jobs recovery in the coming months. The job market for IT professionals mirrors this recent downturn. The number of IT jobs added in May was much lower than expected, according to recent research from management consulting firm Janco. In the short term as is typical during times of economic uncertainty, senior IT managers are looking to IT contractors to support projects rather than hiring into full-time employment positions. The biggest factor is that the skills of unemployed IT workers often don't match what employers are looking for. An IT career requires a lifelong commitment to continuing education and training. Individuals who have failed to keep pace with changes in technology cloud computing, mobile computing, security, unified communications, and social media -- are most often the ones who struggle to stay employed.

Some of the sociocultural factors IT companies will need to be mindful of will be the population shifts that will have a significant impact on economies, companies and customers. The favorable demographic profile of the US will help to spur growth; ageing populations in Europe will inhibit growth. Industries will target more products and services at ageing populations, from investment advice to low-cost, functional cars. Workforces in more mature markets will become older and more female. However, there is growing concern that foreign workers are stealing jobs from unemployed Americans. As far back as 2002, Nobel economics laureate Milton Friedman said that the 1990 H-1B visa program is a government subsidy because it allows employers access to imported highly skilled labor at below-market wages. The excuse is that there are not enough qualified American workers but the reality is that since 1960, 30 million Americans have graduated with bachelor's degrees and advanced degrees, who could work as scientists, engineers, computer programmers and mathematicians.

The landscape looks promising for globalization and networking technologies that will enable firms to use the world as their supply base for talent and materials. Processes, firms, customers and supply chains will fragment as companies expand overseas, as work flows to where it is best done and as information digitizes. As a result, effective collaboration will become more important. The boundaries between different functions, organizations and even industries will blur. Data formats and technologies will standardize. Indian firms will be directly affected by recent changes in Indian tax codes and there is significant uncertainty as US and Indian firm's struggle to adjust to new regulations.
Taxation of offshore deals is likely to increase the cost of acquisitions, and could have a potentially negative effect on

foreign direct investment in India. Tax protection under India's Software Technology Parks program expired in March 2011 and the Obama administration has expressed desire to tax all income earned outside of the United States. Industry structure determines firm conduct and firm conduct work together to determine firm performance. The degree of fragmentation in an industry correlates with the level of competition. The IT consulting industry would appear to follow the structure of Monopolistic Competition. A monopolistically competitive industry is characterized by many firms, a differentiated product, some obstacles to entry, and the basis for raising process for a relatively unique product while retaining customers. The key to understanding this industry structure is that the firms now offer products or services that have unique feature.

This description fits the IT industry perfectly. Many firms compete in this industry, and even the largest firms like Apple, Dell, or HP have less than 20 percent market share. Moreover, while products of one competitor tend to be similar to products of a rival, they are not identical. As a consequence, managers selling a product with unique features tend to have some ability to raise prices when a firm such as Infosys is able to differentiate its product or service offerings, it can carve out a niche in the market in which it has some degree of monopoly power over pricing. Firms frequently communicate the degree of product differentiation through advertising. The consulting industry has global revenues of close to $330 billion in 2008, it grew rapidly (20% annually) throughout the 1980s and 1990s. It is now considered a mature industry that is experiencing low growth or decline (-3.5% in 2009). With over 300,000 "enterprise firms" competing for market share, the market is dominated by a few key players who compete for large client accounts. Technology consulting accounts for 46% of all consulting industry revenues and the activities include design and delivery of computer systems, programming, software solutions, and onsite management.

Being aware of cultural differences is especially important when engaging in international business, as it helps managers understand the national institutions of the host country, why certain business arrangements might be preferred, and how to implement strategies more effectively. To begin to assess the impact of culture we should first point out that when it comes to the dimension of power distance, it is clear that India has a 77/100 ranking indicating a high power-distance culture which would tend to allow inequalities among people to translate into inequalities in opportunity, power, status, and wealth. The United States tends to be more egalitarian, whereas India tends to accept differences in authority and stature. Such a system of authority is embedded in India's deeply rooted caste system. They have a more centralized decision structure and higher levels of supervisory personnel.

In terms of the other dimensions of culture, the U.S. and India seem to rank very close in proximity for Uncertainty Avoidance at 46/100 for the U.S. and 40/100 for India. In the area of Individualism/collectivism, the U.S. which ranks high at 91/100 might present some challenges to an Indian cultural mindset which ranks a 41/100, but not an insurmountable problem since the two cultures have a history of working closely on projects in the IT industry. In the area of masculinity/femininity there are similarities in both cultural approaches. The U.S. ranks 62/100 and India ranks 56/100 indicating that both cultures view the masculine role similarly depending on the industry and the gender of high-ranking officials. When it comes to time orientation, India places a stronger emphasis on persistence, perseverance, and thrift. Whereas, U.S. managers tend to want quick results, which is likely to create different expectations and planning horizons when negotiating contracts. Infosys should provide cultural training for any Indian workers it brings to the United States, to help them adapt to the Americans' fast-paced, results-driven, individualistic and egalitarian work environment. India's competitive advantage currently is its availability of highly skilled, low-cost labor; the financial attractiveness of the Indian economy and business environment; and the ability to import Indian workers into other countries at cost-effective rates.

The most appropriate assessment and answer to this question would have to depend on three factors. (1) Effect of exchange rates in converting Indian Rupee (INR) costs to western currencies. (2) Lower cost of living: In cost of living terms, the salaries of personnel in offshore locations (calculated using the Purchasing Power Parity (PPP) factors. (3) An abundant supply of skilled personnel (of the kind demanded by the offshore model). In any financial P&L where the revenue is in US Dollar (USD), British Pound (GBP) or in Euros and the cost in INR, the conversions of the cost to any of the western currencies deflate the actual cost. As long as the exchange rates undervalue the INR in comparison to its buying power in its domestic market, this cost advantage will continue. In cost of living terms, it is a fact that in the case of experienced IT personnel in India, the salaries, on purchasing power terms, are significantly higher compared to the US and UK. There may even be room for salaries in India to become even more competitive in response to competition from other countries.

As for the abundant supply of skilled personnel that is demanded by the offshore model, their increased availability has been the key driver for the growth of this model. Although projections by analysts indicate that demand will out strip supply as the growth of this model continues, a closer analysis will show that the opposite is more likely. Based on student admissions to IT courses in India, there are signs that the supply of skilled IT personnel will exceed the demand in the next few years.
Infosys Technologies Limited is a leading and billion dollar information technology (IT) firm. The company was founded in 1981 by N.R. Narayana Murthy and six of his friends in Pune, India Infosys headquarters is in Bangalore, India. Infosys international operations grew to nine marketing offices in the United States, and having a presence in Canada, Hong Kong, Sweden, Belgium, France, and Germany. Infosys engages in every aspect of information technology services, ranging from business and technology

consulting to application services, custom software development IT infrastructure services, and business-process outsourcing. As of 2011, many talks among President Barack Obama and Congress about the Visa reform and new tax law changes on international and foreign trade. Some of Infosys's major competitors include Accenture, IBM IT, McKinsey, and HP Enterprises Services. With leading companies as these, we may need to ask the questions of how Infosys gets to the point of profitability. Where does future growth come from? The possibility of a separate company? Partner or merge with a more established consulting firm? Relocate to Ireland for lower corporate tax rates?

Corporate governance is a structure made up stakeholders who will select a management team to run the corporation. There is a bit of variation between stakeholders, management, and supervisory. How the basic structure is implemented into the corporation, depends on from country to country. For Infosys, "corporate governance is about maximizing shareholder value legally, ethically and on a sustainable basis, while ensuring fairness to every stakeholder--customers, employees, investors, vendor-partners, the governments of the countries in which we operate, and the community. Infosys Technologies believes that sound corporate governance is critical to enhance and retain investor trust. They always seek to ensure that they will attain our performance rules with integrity."

Developing a corporate level strategy is the key question: What stages of the industry value chain should the firm participate? Deciding whether to make or buy the various activities in the industry value chain involves the concept of vertical integration. Vertical integration is the company's ownership of its construction of needed inputs or of the channels by which it allocates its outputs. Benefits of vertical integration include securing critical supplies, lowering costs, improving quality, facilitating scheduling and planning, and facilitating investments in specialized assets. Vertical integration risks include increasing costs, reducing quality, reducing flexibility, and increasing the potential for legal repercussions. Strategic outsourcing is an alternative to vertical integration. This involves moving one or more internal value chain activities outside the firm's boundaries to other firms in the industry value chain. What does this all mean? When outsourcing activities outside the home country, it is called off-shoring. Regardless that it is outsourcing or off-shoring, value chain activities tend to grow at a phenomenon rate and speed as opposed staying within or inside of your home boundaries.

Another strategic management idea is leveraging core competencies for corporate diversification. Core competencies are unique skills and strengths that allow firms to increase the perceived value of their product and service offerings and/or lower the cost to produce them. Infosys's ability to provide high-quality information technology services at low cost through leveraging its global delivery model.

Infosys and Wipro are two of the most famous Indian IT service companies that reigns supreme in business process outsourcing, low cost labor, and well-educated English speaking people. Many multinational enterprises have close business with India because of the profitability and sustainability, and not to mention the competitive advantage of outsourcing and technology.

Much controversy with international trading has occurred over the years. It can be an advantage to one firm and a disadvantage to another, depending on who is the home headquarters and whether or not there is international trade, outsourcing and off-shoring. For now, we are concerned with India, the United States, and the tax codes ... where it was and where it is going. In 1991, Infosys and other Indian-based IT companies have benefitted immensely from a tax holiday provided under the Software Technology Parks of India (STIP) plan. Firms engage in software development for export were exempt from paying corporate income tax for up to 10 years, resulting in an overall tax break of ten to twenty percent. The scheme initially expired in 2009, but was extended twice for one year each, pushing the sunset date to March 31, 2011. Despite appeals from Indian IT firms, the Finance Ministry announced in

September 2010 that it would not consider any further extensions. Serious questions about the long-term sustainability of the current off-shore/outsourcing-based business model. Another major change on the horizon is the implementation of India's new direct tax code (DTC) scheduled for April 2012. The direct tax code is a comprehensive tax code designed to replace the 1961 Income Tax Act and a patchwork of other tax laws, which both Indian and foreign businesses find confusing and costly to comply with.

On the flipside of the Indian Tax Code, how about the reform the United States Tax Code? Where does that stand with billion dollar firms? President Barack Obama pointed one problem with the U.S. tax code is that it offers incentives for outsourcing. Reiterating his campaign speech, the U.S. President stated: "The way we make our businesses competitive is not to reward American companies operating overseas with a roughly 2 percent tax rate on foreign profits; a rate that costs taxpayers tens of billions of dollars a year." Furthermore, President Obama's proposal to provide incentives to companies creating jobs inside the United States has further fueled the immigration debate. In fact experts feel that the legislation may actually help Indian firms as they try to become more competitive, whereas the U.S.-based companies that do business in India may be negatively affected. It is during times of crisis that companies come up with some of their most innovative ideas.

Lastly, with the immigration laws and low-cost skilled workers coming to the United States, there is the Reform Act of 2009 with the H-1B and L-1 Visas. The H-1B visa is more valuable, as it is valid for a duration of three years. The L-1 visas are for a much shorter duration and are used by employees who are transferred to the U.S. offices of a company. A true advocate of the immigration laws, Senator Chuck (R-Iowa) and assistant Senate leader Dick Durbin (D-Illinois) introduced a bill to amend the H-1B and 1 visa programs on April 24, 2009. The proposed legislation did not aim to reduce the number of H-1B, but rather contained visions to increase enforcement while discouraging outsourcing. Anti-outsourcing sentiment was at an all-time high door to large-scale job cuts and double digit unemployment in the United States. The legislation never made of committee and was removed from the books when the 112th Congress came into session. Under the so-called "Employ Americans Workers Act," any company that received "Troubled Asset Relief Program funds who applied for H-1B workers had to comply with H-1B dependent rules. The rules stipulated that company must make a good-faith effort to recruit American workers and that it could not replace American workers with H-1B visa holders.

Adrian awakes from her plane ride home from India. Feeling confused and her brain is swimming with questions and thought, her mindless thoughts of the external challenges that lay ahead for the strategy planning committee at Infosys Consulting. What was her first priority? The global competition entering into Infosys backyard? The proposed tax changes to the U.S. and Indian tax codes? Which way was the H-1B visa reform headed? Adrian was wondering what the company was thinking to these possible opportunities and threats.

Future growth, profitability, investment of capital, merge with another company, and relocation -- were topics that struck her in the thought process and needed to be discussed among her group of people before heading back to India. For now, she gathers her items on the plane and forgets about the work that will have to be done, and goes home to settle in from the long trip that just happened and will begin very soon.

Infosys is one of the world's leading IT service firms generating $5 billion in revenues that started with a $250 investment back in 1981 by N. R. Narayana Murphy and six of his friends. Due to the lacking Indian infrastructure, Infosys didn't have the client base needed for their rapid anticipated growth. To compensate they focused their efforts on United States and acquired a contract with Data Basics Corporation in 1983 which allowed them to relocate to Bangalore. Business was going well and Infosys went international by opening an office in Boston, Massachusetts and partnering with Kurt Salmon Associates to aid in marketing their firm. In 1989 the joint venture collapsed leaving the remaining 5 investors filled with uncertainty due to one resigning. Remaining partners rolled up their sleeves and pushed on and thanks to many newly instituted government reforms in India, Infosys began to grow very rapidly. In 1993, Infosys hit the Indian market stock exchange with market capitalization of $10 Million. In 1999, Infosys became the first Indian company to be listed on the U.S. stock exchange. Within one year, their market capitalization grew to $17 billion and had offices all around the world including 9 in the US. Some major clients were General Electric, Reebok International and Holiday Inn.

Today, Infosys conducts business in nearly every aspect of IT including consulting services. They employ 125,000 people between 65 offices and 59 development centers across the world. They are ranked among WIRED magazine's top 40 companies, Bloomberg Business week among top 100 IT and 40 innovative companies and Forbes as top 5 best performing software companies in the world. In India, they are ranked number one as the bet managed company by Finance-Asia. Lately their story hasn't been so pleasant. Infosys, once contemplated as the bellwether of Indian IT industry, has hit a rough patch in the couples of years due to both internal and external factors. The changing landscape of global IT industry has generated a condition of inexact demand, increasing competition, increasing bargaining power of clients, rising attrition amongst the skilled senior employees and lack of employable talent pool in the industry.

Infosys Consulting, their consulting firm, is also crying for help and suffering losses. Using the global delivery model, Infosys takes work to the location with quality talent, lowest risk at the cheapest labor rate. They outsource all of the projects to be completed to the locations with cheap labor while providing on site consultants for their service contracts at a higher rate. By implementing such business approach to complete consulting, Infosys was hoping to have a larger business impact and work directly with business heads who have a lot more say in the direction of a company as opposed to IT managers. So far they have suffered losses and the breakeven point has been pushed back twice due to inability to make profits. Consulting industry is considered to be in the maturity stage of its life cycle. With large competitors such as Jointly, Accenture, Bain, Boston Consulting Group, Booz, IBM Global Services, McKinsey and Monitor owning 25% of the industry revenues, it is incredibly hard to score large accounts that Infosys was looking into with large scale integration.

Recent tax reforms in India and United States alike have the outsourcing companies worried about their futures. In India, up until now, companies were exempt from paying corporate income taxes for 10 years as long as they engaged in software development for export. Until now, only about 7% of Infosys revenue of over $4 billion was taxed at a full rate in India. The new government reform will aid businesses in lowering the post-10-year-grace-period rates but overall it will still increase the amount of taxes paid by all companies. The US tax reform, suggested by President Obama, is to begin taxing off shore revenues as well as on site revenues as long as the company is housed in the US. Even with the tax increases and alterations, it makes sense to continue operation in India, as labor cost is on average 75% lower. Even bigger debate that international companies are facing is the notion of ensuring that American jobs stay in America. This has received a lot of scrutiny and has been battles without resolution for quite some time. Furthermore, there is a reform to the H-1B Visa which will regulate the ability to receive one and place stipulation on businesses hiring such immigrants. As far as we know, it suggest that American citizens are to take priority over H-1B Visa holders and only during a shortage of employees is a company to start hiring such immigrants. A report stated that in 2009 there were 241,000 unemployed IT professionals and the number of employed H-1B Visa holders far exceeded this number. Along with the immense fraud happening at 20%, these visas are being frowned upon more and more each day.

Adrian Patel, who is just returning from her STRAP

conference in India, which is Infosys's annual strategy retreat, has some tough choices ahead of her. She has been assigned to provide strategic guidance for Infosys to overcome the previously mentioned obstacles and ensure tangible bottom-line results. She was confused as to the future direction of the company and where to make significant sacrifices to ensure stability and continued future success.

Considering that the only non-profitable section of Infosys is their consulting business I recommend making it a primary focus. Without considering the US H-1B Visa reform impact on the company and solely focusing on the Indian tax reforms, Adrian must prepare for an inevitable partnership or a loss. Infosys can part ways from their consulting firm and make its own entity so that it doesn't have a negative income effect as it currently holds. This would mean that, if they are unable to sell the consulting firm, they would simply consider that a reduction in assets and downsize the company. Ideally, they should considering selling off the consulting firm while maintaining strong business ties to Infosys IT infrastructure. Perhaps Infosys management and their team are great at IT but they are not so great at managing a consulting firm. It could be as simple as that. It is a problem, however, that the industry is at its maturity level and majority of large portfolios are already working with competition. Attempting at a partnership with another reasonably sized consulting firm with complimenting skill sets would be the ideal option. "The old formula of linear model (cost arbitrage) is no more relevant given the changed scenario, which demands complete business solutions from the IT companies." (Shetty, 2012) A consulting firm that is extremely successful at management but lacking in technology would be a great partner for Infosys considering their current standing. In addition to the partnership, relocation to Ireland of solely the consulting services to reduce the corporate taxes from 30% to 12% could prove to be a long term cost savings.

To address the H-1B visa concern, it will only apply to their US soil based operation. Since Infosys is based out of

India they do possess many employees in the United States that reside and work in the US under such privilege. Due to the astronomical amount of visa holders, Infosys will have to rethink their strategy and relocate their employees to other locations while encouraging the rest to apply for US citizenship. Infosys presence in the US will be drastically impacted and might be forced to close a few locations. What they close here might provide the opportunity to open new locations in places such as Vancouver, Canada, which seems to be a free for all for large companies housing employees that cannot receive legal work status in the US.

The evaluation process of attempting to acquire a partner of Infosys Consulting should begin immediately. Within the first 2 months the paperwork should be drafted to ensure that the company is ready to become marketable. Within 2-6 months, the sales team will venture out and find the highest bidder or to find the best partner to revive the consulting firm. Within 9 months, the sale or acquisition will be completed and all final paper work signed. Within the year, the company should be up and running with their new affiliate begging to draft the plans for future strategic moves for Infosys Consulting.

Exchange rate appreciation is the only likely factor to reduce the cost advantage of offshore. In purchasing power terms, the salaries are at very healthy levels and there is unlikely to be a market-driven push for better salaries driven by awareness of salaries in the west. Supply of personnel will meet the demand as per current trends; there might be some excess supply in the short to medium term which will push salaries down rather than up.

Although there are very prominent firms within the Information Technology (IT) industry, such as IBM IT Services, Accenture, HP Enterprise Services, Deloitte Consulting, and McKinsey, Infosys has been a pioneer in the industry while grossing at least $5 billion annually. Based out of India, Infosys has capitalized on its remote location by providing information technology services by way of consulting and managerial support to countries across the world. It has maintained it competitive advantage by maintaining a close relationship with the cultural effects of the globe onto the industry.

Infosys is one of the World's leading IT service firms, founded in July 1981 by N.R. Narayana Murthy and six other friends in Pune, India. Infosys has come to generate annual revenues nearing $5 billion. Because of India's governmental restrictions, starting a business in that area at that time was nearly impossible. It took Murthy 9 months to get a phone line and three years to gain permission to import computers. Due to India not having an established software development, Infosys was forced to turn to the United States for its software needs. It secured its first U.S. client, Data Basics Corporation, in 1983, and repositioned its headquarters to Bangalore that same year. (Bangalore is known as the Silicone Valley of India due to the high number of IT companies located there). Subsequently, Infosys opened its premiere office in Boston, Massachusetts while joining forces with Kurt Salmon Associates (KSA) in order to market and generate its U.S. operations. Each aspect of the union carried out specific areas of operational management. While Infosys provided the personnel and programming services, KSA solicited for procurement of projects and both companies as a joint venture struggled for several years to succeed. After a long timeframe of governmental suppression, the Indian government implemented economic reforms while removing a majority of the policies and procedures that made social development for many companies nearly impossible, thus making it easier for Infosys and other companies alike to grow more effectively.

Infosys went public by entering the Indian stock exchange in 1993 and then the NASDAQ stock exchange in 1999 thus becoming the first Indian company to be placed within this market. Once Infosys made this choice, it discovered that its market capitalization surpassed $17 billion a year later in 2000 and in turn developed operations internationally in nine marketing offices in the United States, Canada, Australia, the United Kingdom, Japan, Hong Kong, Sweden, Belgium, France, and Germany with accounts with clients such as Holiday Inn, Nestle', Reebok

International, and General Electric. Today, Infosys is engrossed in every feature of IT services, ranging from business and technology consulting to application services, custom software development, IT infrastructure services, and business-process out-sourcing.

In performing a PESTEL analysis of the IT Industry, consideration for the affects that Infosys' external environment has on its performance presents an opportunity to mitigate threats and leverage opportunities. The strategic group in which Infosys falls would be that of Information Technological services within the Technological Industry. The factors within the IT Industry's external environment are political, economic, sociocultural, technological, ecological, and legal in nature. The Political factors affecting Infosys' developmental progress are governmental restraints; the economic factors include the limitations within the domestic and international economies, growth and interest rates, and inflation and deflation; the sociocultural factors are the norms, beliefs, and values of both its immediate society in India and its global society worldwide. Infosys' external environment is also affected by technological factors evolving around the evolution of technology.

Technological progress is persistent and seems to be picking up speed over time with upsurge activity on the internet and advancements in biotechnology and nanotechnology. As purchasing online has radically altered business and consumer behavior, U.S. online retail sales accounted for 6 percent of total retail sales or $140 billion in 2008 and is anticipated to reach 8 percent by 20115. The largest U.S. online retailers are Amazon, Staples, Office Depot, Dell, Walmart, BestBuy, and Hewlett Packard. Leveraging the biotechnology revolution, newcomers like Genzyme or Biogen are now matured pharmaceutical companies. The revolution in nanotechnology is just commencing, but promises major turmoil in a vast array of industries ranging from tiny medical devices to new-age materials from earthquake-resistant buildings.

The ecological effects of Infosys' external environment

are society concerns for the "natural environment, global warming, and maintainable economic growth. Managers con no longer detached from the natural and the business worlds as they are both inseparably linked. BP's notorious oil spill in the Gulf of Mexico following the explosion on the Deepwater Horizon drilling rig may cost the organization an estimated $40 billion. Moreover, the observed failure of BP's CEO, Tony Hayward, to administer the crisis cost him the CEO position, and he was replaced by Bob Dudley. While companies should consider all factors that can potentially adversely affect the companies' ability to maintain its competitive advantage over its competitors, it's more important that the needs and concerns of the community are addressed as well.

The legal factors affecting Infosys' external environment are directly related to the political factors the present guidelines under which the company should operate. In the event that Infosys is unable to perform within the framework of the legal system, its consequences could be costly to its bottom-line. As regulatory changes can affect the outcome of an industry, companies like Infosys should require its managers to maintain awareness of current and future standards in legal requirements in order to implement aspects of these expectations within the creation of its goals and objectives for its business plan. In creating a strategic group map for the IT Consulting Industry, the key dimensions for the horizontal and vertical axis, which identify the distinct differences between the competitors within the market, would be Information Technology (IT) consulting and management consulting. Infosys' ability to formulate and implement a successful strategy for its U.S. consulting arm may be affected by culture in a way that causes Infosys to get directly involved in the way communication techniques are utilized in different cultures and how those cultures perceive how communication should be implemented. As IT consulting is a suitable industry for offshore outsourcing due to it having the characteristic of being effective in outsourcing, this industry presents a sustainable competitive advantage for India being an attractive offshore destination. With the industry having the majority of its employees positioned in various locations in the world, while performing tasks as remotely as overcoming distances greater than the width of the globe, India continues to present with an effective competitive advantage regarding IT services.

Sometime in 2003, the Vice President of Business Practices for United Technologies Corporation, Pat Gnazzo was faced with the challenge of merging over 46,000 new employees gained after the acquisition of Chubb PLC. The challenge outlined the struggle to incorporate these individuals into United Technologies Corporations' global ethics and compliance program. Although Chubb PLC was known to be the United Kingdom based leader in security and fire protection services, United Technologies Corporation had to master the task of integrating this large number of employees as well as bring these individuals up to snuff from Chubb's less compliant ethics practices to United Technologies Corporation's high standard of maintaining ethical guidelines.

United Technologies Corporation has an extensive and complicated history. Once United Aircraft and Transport, the company was created in 1929, when Boeing Airline & Transport combined forced with Hamilton, Sikorsky, Pratt & Whitney, Chance Vought, and Standard Steel Propeller. That same year, the Research Center, the corporation's central research laboratory, established in Connecticut. Due to the United States Government's disapproval, in 1934 the union of United aircraft and Transport was dissolved into three distinct units: Boeing Airplane Company, United Air Lines Transport, and United Aircraft Corporation. Later in 1975, the United Aircraft Corporation changed its name to the United Technologies Corporation, thus the firm into which this writing seeks to study.

Considering the pyramid of corporate social responsibility, it is clear that United Technologies Corporation has economic, legal, ethical, and philanthropic responsibilities to its stakeholders in order to recognize and address the expectations that society has of the business in each of these areas of concern. This framework provides managers with a conceptual model that describes society's expectations and gives guidance towards more effective strategic decisions. According to the decisions made by defense contractors in the 1980s, these actions were breaches of economic, legal, and ethical standards. By exercising questionable acquisition practices, United Technologies Corporation was under fire and accused of fraud, waste, and abuse of government funding, thus taxpayers dollars, above and beyond military spending. This act of overage breaches its economic responsibility due to the lack of consideration for the responsibility to charge appropriately for goods and services, its legal responsibility due to it being unlawful to deceitfully charge more than what a product is valued, and its ethical responsibility due to taking advantage of the trust that the United States government had in its contractors to implement ethical practices and exercise effective self-governance.

The practice of overcharging for goods and services is believed to be widespread due to a lack of governance over such actions, both internally and externally. As overcharges to the United States Government continued well after the scandals revealed during the 1980s and despite industry efforts to self-regulate, the Defense Department implemented ethics and compliance regulatory guidelines in order to protect the United States government from such practices. As United Technologies Corporation implemented self-regulation of compliance within its corporation, it first published its Code of Ethics in 1990 in order to execute standards of conduct over and above compliance with legal requirements, thus influencing the corporate culture to do the same. By maintaining a strict focus on the requirement to maintain the highest level of corporate compliance, United Technologies Corporation executed business practices that were outlined in its policies and procedures manual – the UTC Corporate Policy Manual. The CEO at the time, George David, made it perfectly clear to its stakeholders, managers, and employees that ethics and compliance are our mutual responsibility. We must maintain a spotless, perfect record, period. We are depending on each other. UTC also integrated five major company commitments, performance, pioneering innovation, personal development, social responsibility, and shareowner value. Chubb, on the other hand, presented with a more contrasting framework while being unfamiliar with corporate ethics and compliance, thus causing the VP Gnazzo to first address the challenge of incorporating a workforce that has functioned outside of the compliance guidelines and then the task of training the Chubb workforce into alignment with the established United Technologies Corporation compliance model.

Gnazzo can change the organizational culture of Chubb through training and assessments. The VP should offer training incentives, such as reimbursement for time in study and transportation to/from training sessions, as well as rewards for successful completion of training sessions by way of bonuses and gift certificates. United Technologies Corporation should make the training experience for these acquired employees rewarding and enjoyable. In order to control the degree of carry-over of skills and knowledge, Gnazzo's training team should have frequent assessment periods during the training process in order to measure the effectiveness of absorption and implementation of the new policies and procedures. The training process should include a provisional period of at least 3 years in order for the corporation to monitor whether or not each employee is successful in their implementation of the compliance practice.

Gnazzo should attack the challenge of incorporating the massive workforce acquired by Chubb by ensuring that the acquired employees understand that their presence is valued and that each can make a positive difference in the effectiveness of the corporation's success within its industry. Employee moral will define the degree to which the new staff assumes responsibility for the overall performance of the corporation, which is in line with the modality expressed by United Technologies Corporation's CEO, David George. With these employees having an example to follow, both by words and actions, the probability of congruency between the ethical practices of the United Technologies Corporation and the newly acquired employees is extremely high.

One can tell whether or not a company exercises its ethical promises by the standards that are executed. A company's actions will disclose a company's true intentions thus yielding discovery of how the company truly feels about implementing such social, economic, and legal obligations. A company having daily operations practices in alignment with the promises it makes to its shareholders, managers, and employees, may be the single most influential aspect of a company's performance that can secure its overall success. In conclusion, the United Technologies Corporation appears to be a company that has not only talked the talk but also walked the walk. After having been in the contractual business for the Unites States for nearly 40 years, the United Technologies Corporation has exemplified the idea of taking responsibility for the actions you execute and the environment that has been affected by it. Any company could use UTC as an example of how to prevent ethical fake supporters and how to correct such inadequacies should one occur.

9 CHAPTER NAME
Wal-Mart, Inc.

A unique feature of Wal-Mart retailing is that it is virtually recession proof. In times of economic downturn, consumers flock to discount retailers. During the recession of 1974-1975, sales expanded 42 percent; in the 1981-1982 recessions, sales grew 44 percent; and the recession of 1990's, sales grew 30 percent. As such, Wal-Mart is not affected by economic downturns like many other retailers. Wal-Mart has obtained a distinct competitive advantage by targeting small, rural communities, which leads to lower operating cost this advantage result from lower rents, moderate wages and the absence of unionization. In addition, real estate is significantly cheaper, and smaller communities have a loyal and productive workforce. Although the store location strategy was innovative, several other factors have played a strong role in valuating Wal-Mart the top of the retail mountain. For instance, Mr. Sam's Management practices were even more trend setting than his store location strategy. For example employees are referred to as employees; instead they are called associates. Other factors contributing to Wal-Mart success include rigorous cost control, an excellent distribution Network, and technological advantage. Wal-Mart proudly moves up in Fortune's list of the top ten America's most admired Companies in 200, raising to 5th on the list. Early 2009 Wal-Mart introduced a plan that was hoped to ensure that the company would remain the industry leader. Project Impact is based on three strategic initiatives that will improve the benefits to the customer. The three initiatives are; Save Money, Live Better; Win, Play, Show; and Fast, Friendly, Clean. Wal-Mart is aiming to keep consumers happy and returning to their store once the economy improves. Over the last decade the company had lost customers as they frequented the newer stores of its competitors such as Target. By implementing Project Wal-Mart is renovating its stores in the US by widening the aisles, lowering fixtures, improving signage, and adding natural light to give consumers a store that fees friendlier.

Wal-Mart began with the goal to provide customers with the goods they wanted when and where they wanted them. Wal-Mart then focused on developing cost structures that allowed it to offer low everyday pricing. The key to achieving this goal was to make the way the company replenishes inventory the centerpiece of its strategy, which relied on a logistics technique known as cross docking. Using cross docking, products are routed from suppliers to Wal-Mart's warehouses, where they are then shipped to stores without sitting for long periods of time in inventory. This strategy reduced Wal-Mart's cost significantly and they passed those savings on to their customers with highly competitive pricing. Wal-Mart then concentrated on developing a more highly structured and advanced supply chain management strategy to exploit and enhance this competitive advantage. The main elements of a supply chain include purchasing, operations, distribution, and integration. The supply chain begins with purchasing. Purchasing managers or buyers are typically responsible for determining which products their company will sell, sourcing product suppliers and vendors, and procuring products from vendors at prices and terms that meets profitability goals. Supply chain operations focus on demand planning, forecasting, and inventory management. Forecasts estimate customer demand for a particular product during a specific period of time based on historical data, external drivers such as upcoming sales and promotions, and any changes in trends or competition. Using demand planning to develop accurate forecasts is critical to effective inventory management.

In September 2012, the Indian government announced that it would allow foreign firms to take a majority stake in multi brand retail stores. The opening of India, an emerging economy with a rapidly growing urban middle class, should cause retailers to start salivating. But along with the potential huge opportunity are challenges not only by way of opposition from middlemen and small mom and pop retailers, but also by way of the current state of existing supply chains and infrastructure. Wal-Mart's solution to these two challenges is the direct farm program that it has already implemented for its B2B joint venture with Bhart; they are investing in farmers to help them improve quality and yield and are buying directly from them when possible to aggregate purchases from just a few villages. Specifically, Wal-Mart selects suitable plots of land that are suitable for different types of crops to increase flexibility, selects farmers within the same proximity to reduce logistics costs, and invests in farming techniques modern irrigation systems, seeds, fertilizers, etc.

The idea is that Wal-Mart gives requirements to farmers and purchases directly at a small premium above the prevailing prices from them, thus bypassing middlemen. Currently, Wal-Mart has signed up 6,700 farmers for the direct farm program in India and it plans to scale up this operation to 35,000 by 2015. And in a large, but densely populated country like India, especially in the urban areas, where is there land to create Wal-Mart's big box stores that cover a hundred times more square feet than a typical Indian retailer? Real estate prices in India have shot up many folds in urban areas and in rural areas near cities in recent years, making it expensive to create a store of that size even for a leading foreign retailer. Say for example, that you would like to become a vendor for Wal-Mart; there are many steps that need to be taken. First, find out as much as you can about Wal-Mart, pertinent information about the company's product offerings. You definitely should check your competition. Learn about similar products. Visit your local Wal-Mart and learn as much as you can about their customers as well as the target customer for your product. Second, evaluate your company's ability to be a Wal-Mart vendor. Supplying to a big retailer like Wal-Mart will require that your company have the production, distribution, merchandising capability, financial stability and stamina to make it through this challenging relationship. Take an honest look at your financials to see if your company can afford the opportunity. Every opportunity has a challenge attached to it.

Third, request an optional third party Vendor Evaluation Report to help you assess your company's ability to do business with Wal-Mart and other retailers. Fourth, make sure your business has the appropriate Tax ID Number. Fifth, make sure you have a Universal Product Code (UPC) membership number. This relates to the barcodes you see on every product that is scanned. It also facilitates keeping track of inventory. You will need to submit a letter from the Uniform Code Council detailing your barcode information. Sixth, compile and provide the appropriate information about your product, including pictures for submission. Seventh, Initiate the Wal-Mart Online Product Submission. This application includes all of the information about your product and company. Or, as an alternative have the company to do it for you. The company will help you through the process and "hold your bicycle" until you ask them to let go. For a reasonably small fee, the company can also assess your product or service and complete the documentation process and contact the buyer to request a preliminary review. The Last is step eight, for stage two of the process you will need a Dunn and Bradstreet Number. The DUNCE Number from Dun and Bradstreet (D&B) can be obtained by calling D&B's Customer Resource Center or through their website. The report provides detailed financial information on a supplier's business, including a risk summary and payment trends.

Wal-Mart is the number one retailer in the United States and is at the top of the Fortune 500 listing. Wal-Mart operates in many countries worldwide and is moving into new countries every year. Wal-Mart is also expanding as a retailer. They have expanded into many other sectors of the marketplace, including groceries, gas stations, electronics, and auto maintenance. Each year, Wal-Mart finds new ways to grow and offer more services to their customers. Each year, the number of people who have a stake in Wal-Mart also grows. Each year, more claims are made against Wal-Mart by the unions and other businesses that have been forced out of business. Wal-Mart is often able to uncut many other local industries and more and more local businesses are shutting down when Wal-Mart moves into town. The unions are filing more court claims against Wal-Mart because they encourage their worker not to join unions. As a result of Wal-Mart's ever growing size and variety of services they offer, their public affairs department is going to become more and more important. And as the animosity against Wal-Mart becomes more widespread, here and in foreign countries, Wal-Mart is going to have to work harder to maintain their good reputation. Wal-Mart's foundation will become increasingly more important for giving things back to the community.

How Corporate America Amass Revenue & Growth

CHAPTER 10
SKECHERS USA, Inc.

SKECHERS USA, Incorporation is based in Manhattan Beach, California, designs, develops and markets a diverse range of footwear for men, women and children under the SKECHERS name. SKECHERS footwear is available in the United States via department and specialty stores, Company-owned SKECHERS retail stores and its e-commerce website, and over 100 countries and territories through the Company's global network of distributors and subsidiaries in Brazil, Canada, Chile, Japan, and across Europe, as well as through joint ventures in Asia. A billion-dollar global leader in the lifestyle footwear industry and a high-performance footwear brand, SKECHERS USA, Incorporation designs, develops and markets more than 3,000 styles for men, women and children. SKECHERS' success stems from its employees, high quality, varied product offering, diversified domestic and international distribution channels, and targeted multi-channel marketing.

The company offers two distinct footwear categories: a lifestyle division that includes the charity line BOBS from SKECHERS and a performance division that includes SKECHERS GOrun, SKECHERS GOwalk and SKECHERS GObionic footwear. The company is also rapidly expanding its global business through licensing agreements for fitness and kids' apparel, bags, watches, eyewear and additional merchandise. Internationally, SKECHERS sells its products to department and specialty stores via subsidiaries in Canada, the United Kingdom, Ireland, France, Germany, Spain, Portugal, Italy, Switzerland, Austria, the Benelux region, Brazil, Chile, and Japan, as well as a joint venture with China, Hong Kong, Malaysia, Singapore, and Thailand. SKECHERS also has an extensive network of global distributors that sell its product in over 120 countries and territories, and more than 650 SKECHERS stores around the world.

The marketing mix is a business tool used in marketing and by marketing professionals. The marketing mix is often crucial when determining a product or brand is offering, and is often synonymous with the four Ps: *price, product, promotion,* and *place*; in service marketing, however, the four Ps have been expanded to the Seven Ps or eight Ps to address the different nature of services. SKECHERS USA, Incorporation recognizes that every product is subject to a life-cycle including a growth phase followed by a maturity phase and finally an eventual period of decline as sales falls. Marketers must do careful research on how long the life cycle of the product they are marketing is likely to be and focus their attention on different challenges that arise as the product moves through each stage. Over the last two decades, SKECHERS has grown from a one-style, one-office utility boot business into one of the world's most sought-after footwear brands. A public company with over two billion dollars in annual sales, SKECHERS is a brand in demand by consumers in all time zones. Unique in its approach, SKECHERS prides itself on its varied product offering, unparalleled marketing support, diverse distribution and exciting stores.

The Company is known around the world for designing and marketing stylish, comfortable footwear at a great value. With more than 3000 styles for men, women and children, SKECHERS is a one-stop shop, offering a look for every occasion and need. The Company has grown its presence through an aggressive and targeted approach to marketing and advertising that includes television commercials, print campaigns, magazine placements and outdoor advertisements. With its domestic retail, wholesale, and franchise business moving at full-speed, the Company has exported its business model around the world, successfully developing an international network that includes 10 subsidiaries serving 12 countries, three joint ventures and a network of more than 40 distributors and franchisees. There are now over 550 SKECHERS stores in more than 50 countries across six continents from company-owned locations in iconic destinations like Times Square and London's Oxford Street, to franchised and licensed stores in countries like Canada, Ireland, Spain and Portugal.

The organization continually seek ambitious, experienced international franchisees who share their strategic philosophy and would like to open SKECHERS stores in new and existing markets. Looking for more information. Maintaining brand integrity and its reputation for innovation is a crucial goal in all of SKECHERS' product development and marketing activities. In this video provided in this course, Director of Public Relations Kelly O'Connor discusses her work and the marketing activities that are critical to maintaining SKECHERS' edge in the highly competitive footwear marketplace. All of the market research is done in-house. SKECHERS ' goal is to keep building a global mega brand, through creation of personality and image, a feel, a reputation to translate globally. And so by taking all of the information SKECHERS have from kids in focus groups from all over the world, they bring them back, and that continues to validate what they are doing. SKECHERS does marketing research to evaluate consumer needs. The process by which consumers seek information about products is analyzed when targeting consumers. The methods of information gathering that consumers tend to use at any given step of the buying process help direct companies like SKECHERS to develop effective marketing strategies.

Since its start in 1992, SKECHERS has burnished its image as a maker of hip footwear through a savvy marketing strategy that calls for catering to a closely targeted consumer base. She describes the company's goal of creating a megabrand with an image, personality, and feel that can be translated and marketed globally. SKECHERS has been successful in brand building by means of an "Ask, Don't Tell" approach to product development and marketing: It aims to find out what the market wants and then appeal to customers; wants rather than trying to influence the market with the products that it makes available. The marketer must also consider the product mix. Marketers can expand the current product mix by increasing a certain product line's depth or by increasing the number of product lines. Marketers should consider how to position the product, how to exploit the brand, how to exploit the company's resources and how to configure the product mix so that each product complements the other. The marketer must also consider product development strategies.

At SKECHERS, branding concepts and marketing strategies, the media relations department of the company does a product placement. And together with the Investor Relations team, celebrity placement and artist relations as well as the community relations is done. Media Relations department is basically responsible for the global messaging of the company on what SKECHERS wants to convey to customers, about the company, how SKECHERS say and general translation of these issues is done to customers is done. It is at SKECHERS' corporate headquarters in Manhattan Beach, California, that the head of Media relations helps to direct SKECHERS in identifying customer needs and direct the product to their target markets. To effectively place the right products in consumers' hands at any given moment, SKECHERS seek to address the needs of consumers as directly as possible. SKECHERS learns about its target markets at the same time that it is learning about SKECHERS. While consumers seek information, SKECHERS pay attention to where consumers are looking for products and what kind of products they are seeking. There are four methods of promotion that a company can employ, in informing their market segments. Through personal selling, sales personnel communicate directly, one-on-one with potential customers.

The most effective way to develop message and a brand identity is to commit to a specific portion of the whole market. Target marketing assures that marketing resources are put to the best use by aligning a company to only sell products to the people most likely to purchase them. To act to really separate perspective customers from uninterested parties, SKECHERS must segment the market to divide the total market into smaller markets. The company's target market is the group that is defined by the characteristics that closely match those of the people who most often purchase their products. But how is a market segment identified, especially when the dynamics of a market changes and street credibility. That is the most important thing in order to continuing the life of a brand. Because with a brand, you have to make sure that it's always staying on the edge and it always has that brand integrity. In identifying market segments, companies examine several variables. When marketing shoes, geographical variables might include things like boots being more popular in desert or mountainous regions. Demographic and psychographic variables illustrate the differences between individual consumers, marital status, lifestyle and personal taste. The youth demographic is a lot wider than it used to be, as far as people that consider themselves young and are living that young, youthful lifestyle. So they market to the 12 to 24-year-old primarily. And then really, anyone who wishes that they were in that demographic so it is the younger kids that wish they were 12 and the older people that, you know, love that young, youthful, 24-year-old look. Product use, from SKECHERS' perspective, focuses most fully on brand loyalty and associating SKECHERS' products with the lifestyles it supports. Once SKECHERS has a clear picture of its market and their needs and buying habits, the company tries to make sure that it positions itself where its target market will see it, and they are evaluating alternatives.

The footwear industry is extremely competitive. And the only people that really make it in a big way are the companies that build a brand, first and foremost. And there are very few people. When one thinks about footwear companies, there are very few people that you can think about as a household name that most people know of. With a constant, diligent eye on its market and a dynamic approach to marketing, SKECHERS has positioned itself well to assure that its products will be relevant and its sales robust for years to come. SKECHERS has clearly demonstrated a savvy market analysis by literally walking in the other guy's shoes for a while. Most of the design team whether they be the graphic designers, the product designers, they are actually living that you know the SKECHERS lifestyle. They are out there in the clubs, they come rolling-in in the mornings, but they are out there in the clubs whatever is happening in music they know. They bring to SKECHERS before the mass markets heard about it. They have already gone to the show and have the CDs. Sale promotions are short-term, promotional activities designed to stimulate consumer buying or to entice increased cooperation by strategic partners, such as distributors or retailers. What SKECHERS do is to look towards their employees and look towards the focus groups. The process by which the company make product and brand information available in the most accessible and apparent ways is called promotion.

SKECHERS sells shoes, but they must continually innovate to assure that they are creating products that meet demands of their market. When SKECHERS started the company, it was when utility boots and shoes were really popular. It is when the big leggy shoes and boots were popular. And that was the first introduction. Soon after, they had suede sneakers in the inventory. The whole skate thing was really happening. The whole skate thing was really happening. And then athletic apparel and clothing became popular. And they introduced that in addition to it. And so by doing that, by being on top of the trends, SKECHERS has become a company known for lifestyle footwear and that is cool. SKECHERS must also communicate how their products differ from the competition. The goal of differentiation is to further heighten brand identity and increase competitive edge against similar products. There is no other company in the footwear industry that's been able to successfully provide shoes on a continual basis for men, for women, for kids in the sandal, shoe, boot, sneaker category. There's no one that's been able to do that. And the reason why the company have is because they have invested so much time and money and all of the energy back into building a brand. And they have built a brand that carries lifestyle footwear, cool footwear. And because they have done that, whichever the new category that is being introduced in the market, SKECHERS is able to introduce it as well. SKECHERS USA seeks to learn about their target market at every buying stage. The first consideration consumers make at the point of sale is of the pricing product. SKECHERS assures maximum distribution potential without overreaching its intended target market. In addition to many global channels of distribution through some of the world's strongest established retail chains, SKECHERS now has more than 50 domestic stores stretching from Times Square to Los Angeles's Third Street Promenade.

Once the consumer buys the product, SKECHERS take note of its performance. This stage of post purchase evaluation is integral to the maintenance of a market and the establishment of a brand loyal user base. When this rubber hits the road, SKECHERS is the word on the street. Since 1992, SKECHERS Incorporation USA, a company well known for comfortable footwear with edgy designs, has grown into a globally recognized brand. With distribution in over 110 countries and territories throughout the world, SKECHERS has cultivated a steady expansion in market share against some of the most powerful players in big-dollar product branding, athletic shoe companies, Director of public relations for SKECHERS USA acts as a driving force behind. Basically, SKECHERS' message is simple: They make cool shoes for cool people. And so whatever market SKECHERS is in, that is what they do and they will continue to, from a promotional and product placement standpoint continuing to position they product with cool people, make sure that they have seen in all of the cool places and all of the cool magazines and cool television shows.

In Search of finding ways to improve their manufacturing processes or any type of input/output procedures, large companies are investing lots of time and money into a recently developed practice known as Six Sigma. Six Sigma is an odd term to most people, but to mathematicians the Sigma' is a Greek alphabet letter meaning the sum. In terms of Six Sigma, the sigma refers to standard deviation for statistics, which is used to determine by how much a process differs from perfection. This relates to Six Sigma because the goal of the methodology is to achieve perfection in terms of time and material efficiency. Six Sigma is a business strategy designed to reduce variability in business processes through the elimination of defects. As a result, profitability, efficiency and effectiveness increase. Now embraced by many companies worldwide, the Six Sigma movement has been in existence for almost 30 years. The journey began at Motorola in 1979 when executive Art Sundry's stated in a management meeting, "The real problem at Motorola is that our quality stinks!" The search began for way to eliminate waste from Motorola's processes. Bill Smith, an engineer in Motorola's Communications Sector, is credited as the father of Six Sigma. His pioneering work on defects, first published in 1985, incited significant debate within Motorola on the process of finding and fixing defects. Recognizing a link between fewer defects and lower costs, Motorola set out to incorporate this into their manufacturing processes and Six Sigma was born.

Another Motorola engineer, Mikel Harry, working in the Government Electronics Group, was similarly working on improving quality and joined forces with Bill Smith in 1985. Their work on process capability, tolerance, critical to quality characteristics and design margins laid down much of the foundations of what is modern day Six Sigma. Applying these concepts to Motorola's electronics manufacturing delivered more than $2.2 billion in benefits within four years and $16 billion within 15 years. Motorola CEO Bob Galvin was quick to cite the work of Bill Smith and Mikel Harry in achieving these benefits. Larry Bossidy, newly at the helm of struggling AlliedSignal now Honeywell, saw the results at Motorola and recognized the potential for Six Sigma to help turn the company around. Implementing the program in 1994, Bossidy trained thousands of employees' company- wide in Six Sigma and in the first five years, saved more than $2 billion, bringing the company back from the edge of bankruptcy. Larry Bossidy, in turn, shared the concept with his friend and fellow CEO Jack Welch at General Electric (GE). Perhaps Six Sigma's most well-known proponent, Jack

Welsh drove Six Sigma throughout GE's culture globally beginning in 1995, calling it the most important initiative GE has ever undertaken. General Electric saved more than $12 billion with Six Sigma in the first five years after implementation. Word spread rapidly after GE's adoption of Six Sigma with firms such as Polaroid, Texas Instruments, Ford and Asea Brown Boveri (ABB) rapidly joining the bandwagon. Today, Six Sigma remains part of the corporate culture at firm's worldwide, delivering tangible financial and process benefits.

The objective of the Six Sigma methodology is the implementation of a measurement oriented strategy focused on process improvement and defects reduction. A Six Sigma defect is defined as anything outside customer specifications. Because the outputs of it are not as consistent as they are in manufacturing processes and should not necessarily be expected to be, it will be the responsibility of the ITOG to define the processes, expected outputs, and defects. As a result, through 2007, ITOG's that implement quality management initiatives for example, Six Sigma effectively must do the following three things: Focus process improvement targets on relatively small process areas for example, improving the percentage of changes that were implemented within the authorized change window, rather than trying to improve overall change success. Recognize that integration of required process deliverables for example, problem management requires integration among service desk, problem management, change management, and incident management across a full process may be nearly impossible to measure and may be unmanageable Realize that attempting to achieve 99.9999% accuracy may be too aggressive a goal for most ITOG's.

It was argued in the preceding section that the main competencies that can be built using the Six Sigma program, are an effective creation and utilization of knowledge. The continual effort of Six Sigma projects to understand processes and systems, model them by transfer functions, and define crucial measurements, will result in a better general understanding of how production and service processes work. These competencies enable a superior coordination and integration of processes, learning, and reconfiguration and transfiguration. In order to sustain in a more and more turbulent world a company's resilience becomes all important. Organizations should continually morph their strategy, conform it to emerging opportunities and incipient trends. In order to do so, people all over the organization should be trained in picking up signals.

In order to profit from the competitive advantages that competencies related to Six Sigma can bring, top management should plan the incorporation of these competencies in the organization in such a way that they are difficult to imitate. This involves integrating in and committing to long term paths of competence development: competencies that can be bought on the market or easily built convey no competitive advantage. Thus, companies that invest in Six Sigma training, material and software, and that conduct a number of BB or GB projects will increase their OEE, but companies that commit themselves to the long term trajectory of really integrating the philosophy, attitude and skills of Six Sigma in their organization can use Six Sigma to gain competitive advantage.

An example of such long run trajectory is provided by the General Electric Company. In its annual reports it is stated over and over again that it sees its learning, sharing and action driven culture as its path to sustainable competitive advantage. This vision is stated, for example, in the 1998 Annual Report as follows: That appetite for learning, and the ability to act quickly on that learning, will provide General Electric with what we believe is an unsurmountable and sustainable competitive advantage.

This book studies what strategic benefits implementation of Six Sigma could bring to a company. Six Sigma can do more, however, than eliminate competitive disadvantages. Besides improved OEE, Six Sigma adds a whole range of new capabilities and skills to an organization. These skills could be described as: scientific and disciplined problem solving and decision making behavior, and effective distribution of information over the organization. These skills help tackling the general problem of economic planning under constraints to knowledge. The competencies can be used to leverage a company's competitive strategy. However, when managed well, these competencies have the potential to represent competitive advantages in themselves. An organization that does not merely buy Six Sigma training and conduct Six Sigma projects by the book, but commits itself to a many years trajectory of embedding the Six Sigma attitude and philosophy in the organization, can cash advantages stemming from superior integration of processes, faster learning, and higher resilience.

How Corporate America Amass Revenue & Growth

ABOUT THE AUTHOR

Dr. Ebenezer A. Robinson is an author, professor, mentor, motivational speaker, coach, writer, consultant, researcher, advocate for higher education, and is a California State University Alumnus. He holds an MBA and PhD degree in Business Administration and Electronic Commerce. His call is to educate, motivate, teach, train and empower others for life success. Dr. Robinson has over 30 years of corporate America, government, industry, entrepreneurship, education, consulting, executive director, management accounting, and training experience.

Dr. Prof. Ebenezer A. Robinson is the author of the following books: (1) Financial Prosperity for People and Small Businesses Online: A Case Study, (2) The Principles of Modern Web Design, (3) Omnipresence of Money, and (4) Crime and Consequence.

References:

Anonymous (2005, September). Strategic direction. There is something about Dell Bradford: Vol. 21, Iss. 9; pg. 8, 4pgs Retrieve from 2006http://proquest.umi.com.proxy1.ncu.edu/pqdweb/?index=

Anonymous, (2006). Pass the aspirin. American bankers association. ABA banking journal. New York: Vol.98, Iss. 12; pg. 26, 3 pgs. Retrieved from http://proquest.umi.com.proxy1.ncu.edu/pqdweb/?

Anonymous, (2007). Online banking drops off. Journal of Accountancy. New York: Vol.203, Iss. 1; pg. 14, 1 pgs. Retrieved from http://proquest.umi.com.proxy1.ncu.edu/pqdweb

Anonymous, (2007). Intuit buys Web banker for $1.35B Accounting today. New York: Vol.21, Iss. 1; pg. 1, 2 pgs. Retrieved from http://proquest.umi.com.proxy1.ncu.edu/pqdweb/?

Beckman, A. (2006, January 6). Studebaker overhaul ill-suited in long run http://www.southbendtribune.com/apps/pbcs.dll/article?AID=/20060106/Opinion05/601060438/-1/OPINION/CAT=Opinion05.

Beer, M. and N. Nohria. 2000. Cracking the code of change. Harvard Business Review (May-June): 133-141.

Beu, D. S. & Leonard, N. H. (2004). Evangelism of great works in management: How the gospel is spread. Management decision, 42(10), 1226-1239. Retrieved from http://proquest.umi.com.proxy1.ncu.edu/pqdweb/?

Boone, Tonya (Editor). New directions in supply chain management. Technology, strategy, & implementation. Saranac Lake, NY, USA: Amacom, 2001. p 93-94. Retrieved from http://site.ebrart.com/lib/ncent/doc?

Collier, J.E. & Bienstock, C.C. (2006). How do customers judge quality in an E-tailer? Mit Sloan management review. Cambridge: Vol. 48, Iss. 1; p. 35 Retrieved from http://proquest.umi.com.proxy1.ncu.edu/pqdweb/?in

dex.

Chu, K., (2007). Online banks launch checking accounts: No branches, less paper mean higher interest rates; [Final edition] USA Today. McLean, Va.: pg. B.1 Retrieved from http://proquest.umi.com.proxy1ncu.edu/pqdweb/?did

Citibank (n.d.) My citi. Retrieved from https://web.da-us.citibank.com/cgibin/citifi/scripts/infrastructure/portal.jsp?

Correli, C. (2009). *Ten ways to help employees adapt to change.* Washington, DC 20004: Associated Equipment Distributors, Inc. Retrieved from http://www.cedmag.com/article detail.cfm?id=10925388

Duft, k. D. (n.d.). Management theory and practice: Are there irrevocable Differences? Retrieved from http://www.agribusiness-mgmt.wsu.edu/ExtensionNewsletters/mgmt/mgmttheory.pdf

Delfino, S. (2005). Global perspectives on industrial transformation in the American South. Columbia, MO, USA: University of Missouri Press, p 153.http://site.ebrary.com/lib/ncent/Doc?id=10097294&ppg=165

Ding, S., and Beaulieu, P. (2011). The role of financial incentives in balanced scorecard-based performance evaluations: correcting mood congruency biases. Journal of Accounting Research, 49(5), 1223-1247. doi:10.1111/j.1475-679X.2011.00421.x

Dudra, J. (2010). Legislation affecting green car washing. *Professional Car washing & Detailing,* 34(10), 80.

Easy Being Green. (2008). *Atlantic monthly* (10727825), 301(5), 22.

Gamble J. E. & Thompson A.A. (1999). Dell Computer Corporation: strategy and challenges for the 21st Century. Retrieved from http://www.mhhe.com/business/management/updates/thompson12e/case/dell8.html.

Heathfied, S. M. (n.d.). Top ten ways to retain your great employees. Retrieved from

http://humanresources.about.com/od/
retention/a/more_retention.htm.

Hess, K. L. (1996). The growth of automotive
transportation. Retrieved on from
http://www.klhess.com/car_essy.html

Jana, R. (2007). Reading the new eco labels. Businessweek
Online, 24.

Jick, T. D., & Peiperl, M. (2011). *Managing change, text and
cases.* (3rd ed.). McGraw-Hill.

Kapuscinski, R., Zhang, R. Q., Carbonneau, P., Moore, R. &
Reeves, B. (2004). Inventory decisions in Dell's supply
chain. Linthicum: Vol.34, Iss. 3; pg. 191, 15 pgs. Retrieved
from
http://proquest.umi.com.proxy1.ncu.edu/pqdweb/?index.

Rothaermel, R. T. (2013). *Strategic management: Concepts
and cases.* New York, NY: McGraw-Hill.

Kumar Ashok (2001). Perspective: Dell's high-stakes storage
Gambit Retrieved from
http://news.com.com/Dells+high-
stakes+storage+gambit/2010-1071_3-281546.html.

Loepp, D. (2012). Green guides seek details on claims.
Plastics News, 24(30), 0006.

Laudon, K. C. and Traver, C. G. (2006). E-Commerce,
Business, Technology, and Society (3rd Ed.). Prentice
Hall. Upper Saddle River, New Jersey.

Lu, M., Liu, C., Jing, J., and Huang, L., (2005). Internet
banking: strategic responses to the accession of WTO by
Chinese banks Industrial Management
Data Systems. Wembley: Vol. 105, Iss. 3/4; p. 429.
Retrieved on from http://proquest.umi.com.proxy1

Maney, Kevin (2003). USA Today. Dell business model turns
to muscle as rivals struggle Retrieved from
http://www.usatoday.com/money/
industries/technology/2003-01-19-dell-cover_x.htm

Martin Davis. (2012). Change management - cracking the
code of change. Retrieved from
http://www.enterprisecioforum.com/en/blogs/mdavis1
0/ch ange-manaement-part-1-cracking-code

Malhotra, Yogesh (Editor). Knowledge management and

virtual organizations. Hershey, PA, USA: Idea group publishing, 2000. p 155-156. Retrieved from http://site.ebrary.com/lib/ncent/Doc?id=

McCarthy, P. (2002). *Brief Outline of the History of I/O Psychology* Retrieved from http://www.mtsu.edu/~pmccarth/io_hist.htm

Management history (n.d.) Retrieved from http://telecollege.dcccd.edu/mgmt1374/book_contents/ loverview/management_history/mgmt_ history.htm

Montagna, J. A (2006). The industrial revolution. Retrieved from http://www.yale.edu/ynhti/curriculum/units/1981/2/81 .02.06.x.html

Orr, B., (2004). E-banking job one: Give customers a good ride. American bankers association. ABA banking journal. New York: Vol.96, Iss. 5; pg. 56, 2 pgs. Retrieved from http://proquest.umi.com.proxyI.ncu.edu/pgdweb/

Orr, B., (2004). Me to me payments are ready for prime time. American bankers association. ABA Banking Journal. New York: Vol.96, Iss. 7; pg. 62. Retrieved from http://proquest.umi.com.proxy1.ncu.edu/pqdweb/?did

Parks, C. A. (n.d.) Management pioneers: Women as early contributors to the Management discipline. Retrieved from http://www.westga. edu/~bquest/2001/women.htm.

Pr, N. (2011). Green earth technologies' G-clean™ super concentrated products   now certified by the home depot® eco options™ program. PR newswire U

Porter, G. (2005). Industrial revolution. Retrieved from http://encarta.msn.com/encyclopedia_761577952_2/In dustrial_Revolution.html

Nelson, D. (1999). The scientific management of labor. Retrieved from http://gozips.uakron.edu/~nelson/scimgtla.htm

Sarel, D., and Marmorstein, H., (2004). Marketing online banking to the indifferent consumer: A longitudinal analysis of banks' actions. Journal of financial services

marketing. London: Vol.8, Iss. 3; pg. 231, 13 pgs.
Retrieved from
http://proquest.umi.com.proxy1.ncu.edu/pqdweb/?
Sugrue, T. J.(n.d.). Automobile in American life and society
from motor city to motor metropolis: How the
automobile industry reshaped urban America. Retrieved
from http://www.autolife.umd.umich.edu/ /Race/R
Overview/R_Overview.htm
Stanley, T. L. (2004, November). Understanding
management progress. Supervision 65(11),
12-15. Retrieved from
http://web.ebscohost.com/ehost/detail?
Seven steps to success through people (n.d.). Retrieved from
http://www.motivationnetwork.com/article34#2
Second industrial revolution (2006). Retrieved from
http://en.wikipedia.org/wiki/Second_Industrial_Revol
ution
Steam engine (2006). Steam Engine. Retrieved from
http://en.wikipedia.org/wiki /Steam_engine
Strickland, N. (2001). A history of cotton mills and the
industrial revolution Retrieved from
http://narvellstrikland1.tripod.com/cottonmill
history2/index1.html.
Spooner, J. G. (2004). Rollins to take up the reins at Dell
Staff Writer, CNET News.com Retrieved from
http://news.com.com/Rollins+to+take+up+the+reins+a
t+Dell/2100-1003_3-5271423.html.
Taylor, F. W. (1911). The principles of scientific management.
New York: Harper Bros., Retrieved from
http://www.fordham.edu//halsall/mod/1911taylor.html
The scientific management era (2004) Retrieved from
http://faculty.ncwc.edu/TOConnor/417/417lect03.htm.
Wolek, F. W. (2004). The lesson of guild history: Variance
reduce must be balanced with innovation. The quality
management journal.
Wolfe D., (2007). In Brief: Online Resources in Cell Phone
Banking. American Banker. New York, N.Y.:
Vol.172, Iss. 2; pg. 9. Retrieved from
http://proquest.umi.com.proxy1.ncu.edu/pqdweb/?

Wren, D. A. (2005). The history of management thought (5th Ed). New Jersey: John Wiley Sons, Inc. 9-72.

How Corporate America Amass Revenue & Growth